# JUDITH

Edited by
Henry R. Cooper, Jr.

EAST EUROPEAN MONOGRAPHS, BOULDER
DISTRIBUTED BY COLUMBIA UNIVERSITY PRESS, NEW YORK
1991

TRANSLATED FROM THE CROATIAN BY
HENRY R. COOPER, JR.
INDIANA UNIVERSITY

Dedicated to Professor Emeritus
Ante Kadić
On the Occasion of
His Eightieth Birthday,
18 January 1990

# LIBAR
## MARKA MARULA SPLIĆANINA
U KOM SE UZDARŽI ISTORIJA SVETE UDOVICE

# JUDIT
U VERSIH HARVACKI SLOŽENA
KAKO ONA UBI VOJVODU OLOFERNA
POSRIDU VOJSKE NJEGOVE
I OSLOBODI PUK IZRAELSKI
OD VELIKE POGIBILI

THE BOOK OF
MARKO MARULIĆ OF SPLIT
IN THE WHICH IS CONTAINED
THE HISTORY OF THE HOLY WIDOW

JUDITH

COMPOSED IN VERSE IN CROATIAN,
CONCERNING HOW SHE DID SLAY
THE CHIEF CAPTAIN HOLOFERNES
IN THE MIDST OF HIS ARMY
AND DID FREE THE PEOPLE OF ISRAEL
FROM GREAT PERIL

# TRANSLATOR'S FOREWORD

"The History of the Blessed Widow Judith," composed in 1501, published only in 1521, by Marko Marulić (1450-1524), a pious layman and world-renowned Latinist of the Dalmatian city of Split, is the first major work of modern Croatian literature. It is based closely on the apocryphal or deuterocanonical Book of Judith in the version translated into Latin by St. Jerome for inclusion in the Vulgate (readers of the Authorized [King James] Version of the Bible will note certain small discrepancies between their Judith and the Vulgate's, due to the differing provenience of the translators' sources). "The History of the Blessed Widow Judith" was composed in the Čakavian dialect of what is now known as the Serbo-Croatian or Croato-Serbian language, but a Čakavian so distant from the contemporary dialect of that name still spoken along the Dalmatian coast of Yugoslavia, and so replete with alien elements (one commentator cites words from Italian, German, Turkish, Latin, Hungarian, as well as the other major dialects of Serbo-Croatian, Kajkavian and Štokavian[1]), that it is for all practical intents and purposes incomprehensible to the average modern speaker of Serbo-Croatian. Despite the linguistic difficulties, however, "Judith" has played a seminal role in the development of Croatian literature, and no era, including the present, in the five-hundred year history of Croatian letters has been exempt from its influence or immune to its charms. Com-

---

1. Marin Franičević, in his introduction to Marko Marulić, *Versi harvacki* (Split: Čakavski sabor, 1979): 48-9. This version of "Judith," edited by Marin Franičević and Hrvoje Marović, designated Book 2, Volume 1 in the series *Humanisti* of the Splitski književni krug, under the general editorship of Cvito Fiskovića, is the basis of the present translation and the source of the original text on each left-hand page. I am also deeply indebted to the translation into the modern Croatian literary language by Marko Grčić in Marko Marulić, *Judita* (Zagreb: Mladost, 1983), though here and there I disagree with some of the solutions proposed by him for Marulić's less comprehensible verses. Also of great use, and the basis for Grčić's translation, is the version of "Judith" published by Ivan Slamnig in the series *Pet stoljeća hrvatske književnosti,* Vol. 4: Marko Marulić, *Judita, Suzana, Pjesme* (Zagreb: Matica Hrvacka, Zora, 1970). For a very thorough examination of Marulić's life in English based on then recent discoveries in the Split archives, see Mirko A. Usmiani, "Marko Marulić (1450-1524)," *Harvard Slavic Studies* 3(1957): 1-48.

bining in itself many of the characteristics that would typify subsequent Croatian literature–an unambiguous Roman Catholic orientation, a love for the spoken language, particularly in its dialectal forms, a strong feeling for the poetic phrase, the articulation of an embattled mentality, and an appreciation of Croatia's special role as *Antemurale Christianitatis* in European culture–Marulić's "Judith" is a microcosm of the only South Slavic literary tradition to enjoy continuous growth and development.

To be appreciated by a reader outside the Croatian literary tradition, "Judith" must be approached with care, from a variety of directions. First it should be apprehended synchronically, as poetry, though this is virtually impossible to do if one operates only with a translation. In its original language its poetic elements are obvious. Its six books are composed of 2,126 dodecasyllabic verses, with a regular, strong caesura after the sixth syllable. In each couplet, the first hemistich rhymes with the third, the second with the fourth, and the rhyme of the even-numbered hemistichs furnishes the rhyme for the odd-numbered pair in the following couplet. By and large the rhymes are feminine, and often grammatical in origin. The meter is mixed trochaic and dactylic. It must be admitted that over the long haul the utter regularity of the meter becomes somewhat monotonous. Yet the poem is saved from being boring by the colorfulness of its imagery, and the cleverness (sometimes even archness) of the poet in manipulating words and phrases to enliven the verse. I have despaired of translating most of this linguistic playfulness into English, though I have tried to retain some of the color of the Croatian original in a variety of ways. For one, I have attempted to imitate the language of the King James Version of the Book of Judith: though archaic to the modern English ear, this idiolect is still understandable, and conveys a flavor and dignity that are quite similar, in my opinion, to Marulić's own language vis-à-vis modern Serbo-Croatian. Second, though I have sought throughout to be accurate, here and there I have not shied away from improvising colorful equivalents to render the spirit, if not the literal meaning, of the original. Finally, I have attempted to the extent of my own abilities and the resources of the thesaurus to incorporate as much of the lexical riches of English in the poem as possible. Marulić's language, in keeping with his Biblical source and Renaissance models, is somewhat circumscribed, but through his use of Slavic prefixes and suffixes, which on occasion reaches the extreme limit of the language, he has obviously attempted to expand on his limited supply of root words. Etymological parallels failing in English, I have sought equivalents in the vastly larger English lexicon.[2] The bulk of the verse in "Judith" is narrative: for the most part it hews very closely to the Vulgate text. Occasionally the narrative is interrupted by the speech of a principal character: here too Marulić has in essence translated his Latin original into Croatian. Only certain descriptive passages, where additional details are invented to heighten the dramatic effect of a scene, or the infrequent direct addresses to the reader by the poet, depart significantly from the Bible: many critics find in these verses the true beauty and originality of the poem.[3] In all fairness to Marulić, however, both his poeticizing and "Croaticizing" of the Latin prose are masterful: no seams appear where he has joined his own words to the original text, there are no compromises to avoid difficulties. "Judith" moves along at a steady, stately pace throughout. In my opinion Marulić's real achievement lies in his faithfulness, not only to the tale of Judith itself, but also to the linguistic system into which he was transposing it. His Croatian "Judith" has an integrity of voice which bespeaks true poetic genius.

As the first sustained artistic writing in Croatia, "Judith" has profound historical value as well. Though it was not the first vernacular work of Croatian literature–Marulić himself in the introduction to "Judith" speaks of *naši začinjavci,* that is, "our composers," who preceded him in the matter of verse writing in Croatian–nevertheless it can claim primacy for the high seriousness of its purpose and tone. Very much in the style of his contemporaries in Italy, Marulić imbued his work with the rhetoric of the Renaissance: by appealing to them in their native tongue, he sought to persuade his fellow citizens to amendment of life, reform of morals, and resistance to evil, particularly the evil that was literally at the gates of Split and all the other cities of Dalmatia, the infidel Turk. The Biblical heroine Judith was for Marulić the epitome of the few and feeble withstanding and even conquering the numerous and strong. Judith's success derived not from her strength and only partially from her beauty: both the Bible and Marulić make it abundantly clear that her victory was the result of her resourcefulness, faithfulness and purity of life. Marulić, whose lifespan coincided with the Turkish deluge of

---

2. For a complete list of all of the Croatian words Marulić used, see Milan Moguš and Željko Bujas, *Kompjutorska konkordancija Marulićevih djela* (Zagreb: Zavod za lingvistiku Filozofskog fakulteta Sveučilišta, 1980).
3. See, for example, Slamnig, op. cit., p. 20.

Southeastern Europe-the Ottomans took Constantinople three years after he was born, and would be at the gates of Vienna five years after his death-had no illusions about armed resistance to the Muslim onslaught, at least resistance on the part of his fellow-countrymen standing alone. His "Judith" is not a call to arms per se, and Marulić was not a warrior. Rather he was a devout Roman Catholic, and he understood moral rearmament to be the most effective defense against an enemy whose threat was spiritual as well as military. Therefore his "Judith" is a summons to repentence and renewal on the part of a populace whose faith he felt to be insufficient for the mighty task at hand. It is very much a Lenten tract, a fact to which Marulić alludes in the first words of his introduction. Perhaps herein lies the reason for the work's enduring appeal: though the Turks are no longer a threat, the moral and ethical dilemma posed in "Judith," the conflict between overpowering evil and the faithful few, is alive to the present day.[4] As one of the many astute Yugoslav critics of Marulić notes in his introduction to a modern rendering of the poem,

> In regard to that entity [*amplitudu*] called the five hundred years of Croatian literature, Marulić stands in post position, both as a poet and as a prose writer, for he was a lyricist, epic poet, translator and recaster of poetry, an essayist, theoretician, even a polemicist. The farther we recede from him, it seems, in view of the recent, genuine interest in him, the nearer to us he appears to be.[5]

Finally a word about the texts presented in this volume: each left-hand page contains a slightly adapted version of Marulić's 1521 publication of "Judith." As Franičević notes in his afterword,[6] the

---

4. See Vladimir Filipović, "Osnovi etičko-filozofske orijentacije Marka Marulića," in: *Zbornik u proslavu petstogodšnjice rodjena Marka Marulića, 1450-1950* (Zagreb: Jugoslavenska Akademija Znanosti i Umjetnosti, 1950): 281-98. According to Professor Miroslav Pantić (University of Belgrade), not all copies of this collection contain this article: for a variety of reasons it was expunged and replaced by Vjekoslav Štefanić's article, entitled "Još Marulićevih stihova," on exactly the same pages. I am very indebted to Professor Pantić for bringing this article to my attention, and giving me a copy of it.
5. Mirko Tomasović, "Marko Marulić Marul," in Marko Marulić, *Judita* (Translation and Commentary by Marko Grčić), op. cit.: 193.
6. Marulić, *Versi harvacki,* op. cit.: 345-8.

only important alterations involve the use of the accented letters ć, č, š and ž for Marulić's (often inconsistent) graphic conventions rendering these sounds, the introduction on some occasions of j, and the omission of h (or its occasional replacement with k) in some word-initial situations. On the other hand Franičević has preserved Marulić's ar where most modern editions have replaced this with syllabic r: as he points out, in this spelling Marulić was untypically consistent, so that the digraph probably reflects Marulić's pronunciation accurately. The same is true of modern lj and nj: as appropriate, these are separated by an apostrophe (so l'j and n'j) to reflect the presumed lack of assimilation in Marulić's Čakavian (so for example, in the first verse: *hvaljen'ja*). Editorial judgment, finally, has been used where v and u (*mev* vs. *meu* [modern Serbo-Croatian *medju*]), s and š, seem inconsistently differentiated in the original.

The arrangement of the Croatian text reflects Marulić's use of a capital letter at the beginning of each verse (modern Serbo-Croatian would normally have a lower-case letter). Since initial capitals are the norm in English, this practice has been followed in the translation. On the other hand, the Croatian text is divided into quatrains (verse one being flush with the left margin, verses two, three and four indented), to stress the rhyming pattern of Marulić's poetry: aλλbb, aλλbb, bλλbc, bλλbc (where the first letter represents the rhyme of the first hemistich, the second the final rhyme of the verse). The English translation avoids this division (since no attempt has been made to duplicate the rhyme), but to facilitate comprehension it has added paragraph divisions. Punctuation has, of course, been modernized on both the left and right pages according to modern usage. One last point: Marulić spelled God (Serbo-Croatian *Bog*) with a lower-case b, as was the custom in his time; Franičević has capitalized the word, as is the custom in ours.

In preparing this translation, I have incurred many debts to many individuals and institutions. First and foremost I would like to express my thanks to the Andrew W. Mellon Foundation for its generous support, administered through the Russian and East European Institute of Indiana University, during the summer of 1985. In granting me the luxury of two months' worth of concentrated, consecutive hours in which to think and read, it gave the work at hand a tremendous impetus, one which has carried it forth to its conclusion now. I am also most grateful to the Office of International Programs of Indiana University for selecting me to take part in Indiana's fruitful exchange with the University of Zagreb in May 1985: were it not for the opportunity afforded me then to consult directly with Yugoslav scholars involved with Marulić, my work on the poem would have been much more difficult and time-consuming. For the assitance of friends and colleagues in Yugoslavia I am also indebted, particularly to Mr. Marko Grčić, who read and commented on my translation most helpfully; Professor Marija Mitrović of the University of Belgrade; and Professors Milan Moguš and Željko Bujas of the University of Zagreb; to Mrs. Emilija Beltram of the Komitet za prosvjetu SR Hrvatske; and to the Admiñistration of the University of Zagreb, whose cooperation, kindness and hospitality made my stay in that city so productive. Finally I would be remiss if I did not express my gratitude to my friend and colleague, Professor Emeritus Ante Kadić of the Department of Slavic Languages and Literatures of Indiana University, for his persistant encouragement of my labors, his generosity in sharing his many insights into Marulić with me, and for his careful reading of the first book of the translation. It is to him, on the happy occasion of his eightieth birthday, that I dedicate this volume. While I take the responsibility for infelicities and errors in my version of "Judith" upon myself alone, I delight in sharing the honor of bringing this important work into English with those named above and others who have assisted me in the endeavor.

Henry R. Cooper, Jr.
Bloomington, Indiana
2 June 1990

# JUDITH

### POČTOVANOMU
U ISUKARSTU POPU I PARMANCIRU SPLICKOMU
### GOSPODINU DOM DUJMU BALISTRILIĆU
KUMU SVOMU
### MARKO MARULIĆ
UMILJENO PRIPORUČEN'JE
S DVORNIM POKLONOM
MILO POSKITA

1    Sih dan svetih korizmenih, počtovani u Isukarstu gospodine i kume moj dragi dom Dujme, privraćajući ja pisma staroga Testamenta, namirih se na historiju one počtene i svete udovice Judite
5    i preohologa Oloferna, koga ona ubivši, oslobodi svu zemlju izraelsku jur od nadvele pogibili. Tuj historiju čtući, ulize mi u pamet, da ju stumačim našim jazikom, neka ju budu razumiti i oni ki nisu naučni knjige latinske aliti dijačke. Da od
10    te stvari hoteći tvomu otačastvu, obojega jazika dobro umiću, dar prikazati, odlučih naslidovati hitrost dice one ki o mladom litu starijih svojih darijući, naranče nadiju mirisnimi zel'ji, mažuranom, rusmarinom, rutom; umitelno naprave

# TO MY REVEREND FATHER IN JESUS CHRIST, THE DEAN OF SPLIT, MY LORD DON DUJAM BALISTRILIĆ, MY GODFATHER, MARKO MARULIĆ THIS MODEST GIFT WITH COURTLY OBEISANCE PRESENTETH

During these holy days of Lent, my Reverend Lord in Jesus Christ, and my Godfather, Dear Don Dujam, whilst leafing through the books of the Old Testament, I came upon the history of that honourable and holy widow Judith and of the arrogant Holofernes, how she did, having slain him, liberate the whole land of Israel from the peril which did overshadow it. In reading this history I was minded to translate it into our tongue, so that it might be understood by them who are not learned in the Latin or clerical writing.[1] That of this matter I might make a gift to my Reverend Father, who knoweth both of these languages well, I resolved to imitate the cunning of children who, making presents to their elders at the new year, clothe their oranges with fragrant herbs, marjoram, rosemary, rue; cleverly do they arrange

---

1. The Croatian here, "ki nisu naučni knjige latinske aliti dijačke," Grčić translates as "who are not accustomed to either Latin or Italian books." Following *Versi harvacki,* I have understood "latinske aliti dijačke" (or "djačke") as equivalents, "Latin or [as we sometimes call it] clerical writing," rather than as contrastives, "[either] Latin or Italian." (See too Book Six, verse 341, where "djački" clearly means "in Latin," since it refers to the Latin word *holocausta,* which in Italian would be *olocausti.*) In this way then the following line, where Marulić speaks of Balistrilić's knowing "both languages" well, means that he knows Latin and Croatian, not Latin and Italian. For him Marulić does not therefore have to translate the Book of Judith, since he can read it in the original and make his own translation into Croatian, but he does have to adorn it, to make his gift more acceptable.

dar svoj, da zloćudo loveći poveksě uzdarje. Ja
put zloćudi njih ne perim, da samo onogaj hitra
kićen'ja; jer inoga uzdarja od vas ne išćem, nego
kô sam vele od pri našao: ljubav pravu i svaršenu
u Isukarstu, kû mi stanovito nosite veće ner
sam dostojan, da koliko se pristoji pitomšćini
vašoj kâ svakomu prikloniti i prijaznivi. Tu poni
hitrost — kako dim — naslidujući, usilovah se
rečenu historiju tako napraviti, kako bude nikimi
izvanjskimi urehami i uglajen'jem i ulizan'jem i
razlicih masti čirsan'jem obnajena; a to, da ne
rečete da vam poklanjam onuje žita rukovet koju
u vaših knjigah bolju nahodite. Zaisto je onaje
rukovet da mnozim cvitjem opkićena; kada ju
dobro razgledate, reći ćete: prominila je lice,
kakono voćna stabla premaliti kada najveće ve-
selo cvasti budu. Evo bo historiju tuj svedoh u
versih, po običaju naših začinjavac, i jošće po
zakonu onih starih poet, kîm nî zadovoljno poči-
tati kako je dilo prošlo, da mnoge načine opkla-
daju, neka je vičnije onim ki budu čtiti, nasli-
dujući umitelnu sredbu raskošna kuhača ki na
gospockoj tarpezi ne klade listo varene ali pečene
jistvine, da k tomu pridaje šaprana i paprana i
inih tacih stvari, da slaje bude onim ki su prišli
blagovati. Ništar manje, da prem dar moj nî
tolika dostojanstva, uzdan sam u vašu dobrotu da
ćete ga ljubeznivo prijati ćića priproste pitom-
šćine i sarčene prijazni kâ je od davna meju
nami. Eto k vam gre Judita gospoja mâ visoko
počtovana, more biti ne s manjom urehom nego
kada se ukaza Olofernu, ne da vas kako i njega
tim prihini, da prija pokripi u uzdržan'ju svete
čistoće, prid oči vaše ponesši i postavivši sve
lipote, krasosti, kriposti, dike i slave svoje, kimi
se je urešila vele plemenitije i gizdavije nego kê
no se reše svilom, zlatom i biserom; a znajući da
će moći tako počteno pribivati pod strihom va-

their gift that through craft they might receive all the greater gifts in return. I aspire not to their craftiness, but only to that clever adornment; for no other reciprocation do I seek from thee, than that which I have oftimes encountered before: affection true and perfect in Jesus Christ, which thou bearest for me in greater measure than I deserve, but which befitteth thy nobility, inclined and amiable as it is to each and every one. Imitating thus this cunning, as I have said, I did struggle to fashion the said history so that it might be adorned with certain patent charms and refinements and embellishments and a varnish of varied hues; all this that thou mightest not say that I am offering thee that clutch of grain which thou findest more readily in thine own books. Verily this clutch is decked about with many blossoms; when thou regardest it well, thou shalt say: it hath changed its aspect like the fruit trees in spring when they most joyously shoot forth. For behold, I have composed this history in verse, in the manner of our predecessors[2] and according to the law of those ancient poets who thought it not sufficient to relate how a matter occurred, but they did circle it about with many deeds, that it might be the more pleasant to them that read it; following thus the clever practice of the generous cook who on his master's table placeth not merely boiled or baked dishes, but addeth to them saffron and pepper and other such things, that they might be more appetizing to them who have come to dine. In no less manner, though my gift be not of such great dignity, do I trust in thy goodness that thou wilt accept it kindly out of the simple gentleness and heartfelt friendship that have been between us for many years. Behold my highly honoured lady, Judith, cometh to thee, with perhaps no less charm than when she appeared before Holofernes, not that she might therewith seduce thee as she did him, but rather that she affirm thee in the maintenance of saintly purity, having brought before thine eyes and displayed all her beauty, grandeur, virtue, merit and glory, with which she hath adorned herself more nobly and proudly than those who dress in silk, gold and pearls; and knowing that she might so honourably dwell beneath thy roof

---

2. In the Croatian, "po običaju naših začinjavac": Slamnig, in his introduction to Volume 4 of *Pet stoljeća hrvatske književnosti* (op. cit.: p. 19), claims that the verb "začinjati" means "to perform, improvize rhymed songs/lyrics in the people's language, in meters not classic." "Začinjavac," the noun derived therefrom, might then be translated as troubadour, jongleur, minstrel. While I do not disagree with Slamnig on this matter, I have prefered a more neutral term, which however accurately reflects the point, that Marulić is following both his own Croatian poetic predecessors, whatever their manner or style might have been, and the poets of old, who obviously did write in classic meters.

šom kako je nigda pribivala u Betuliji pod svojom. Kada se budete s njom pitomo razgovarati,
55 daržu da ju ćete pohvaliti ne manje ner veli pop Eliakim ki od Jerosolime dojde sa svimi leviti u Betuliju vidit ju, čuvši sarca sminost, dila hrabrost i čudnovatu svetinju života nje. S toga joj dâ hvale izvarsne, časti dostojne, uzvišen'je visoko
60 i poljubljen'je čisto, duhovno, pobožno, nijednom trohom nedostojna poželin'ja ockvarnjeno, kako se svetim pristoji i slugam božjim podoba. I vi poni dvorno ju primite, dobrovoljno nastanite, i kû vazda hvalite dilom, tu pohvalite i ustmi; jer
65 je naučna hvaljena biti, navlastito od svetoga reda vašega popovskoga. Nju primite, a meni zapovijte: zapovidem vašim služba mâ vazda je pripravna da izvarši ča budete veliti, koliko joj bude uzmožno. Mir i milost gospodina našega
70 Isukarsta budi vazda s vami. Amen.

Od rojen'ja Isukarstova u pùti godišće parvo nakon tisuća i pet sat, na dvadeset i dva dni miseca aprila. U Splitu gradu.

as once she did dwell in Bethulia 'neath her own. When thou dost gently engage her in conversation, I wager that thou wilt praise her no less than did the high priest Joakim[3], who came from Jerusalem with the Levites to see her, having heard of her heart's bravery, her deeds' nobility and the remarkable sanctity of her life. For that did he give her excellent praise, fitting honours, high exaltation and affection pure, spiritual, pious, unbesmirched by e'en one drop of unwholesome desire, as befitteth the saints and suiteth the servants of God. Therefore do thou also receive her, accommodate her willingly, and whom thou dost always praise in deed, praise her now also with thy lips; for she is accustomed to be praised, most especially by thy holy priestly caste. Receive her, and command me: by thy commands is my service always prepared to execute what thou shalt ordain, as far as it be able. The peace and grace of Our Lord Jesus Christ be with thee always. Amen.

From the birth of Jesus Christ in the flesh, the first year after one thousand and five hundred, on the twenty-second day of the month of April, in the City of Split.

---

3. The Standard (King James) Version, speaks of only one high priest, Joacim (Judith 4:6 and 15:8). The Vulgate speaks in 4:6 of "sacerdos . . . Eliachim" and in 15:9 of "Ioacim . . . summus pontifex." Marulić refers only to "Eliakim, veli pop"; for simplicity's sake, I have called him Joakim (the modern spelling) throughout. By and large, however, I have maintained the spellings of the Standard Version (thus "Nabuchodonosor" for the modern "Nabuchadñezzar," etc.).

ISTORIJA SVA NA KRATKO

*kâ se uzdarži u ovih knjigah*

Nabukodonosor, kralj od Babilonije i od Asirije, daržeći tad grad Ninive, pobi Arfaksata, kralja od Medi, kon rike Eufrata. Posla k mejašnikom svojim da se podlože njemu: podložit se
5 ne htiše. Otpravi s vojskom svoga vojvodu Oloferna, ki kuda projde, sve obuja. Pride napokon u zemlju izraelsku. Bi velik strah po svoj zemlji. U Jerosolim činiše mnoga poniženʼja i posvetilišća, Bogu se priporučujući. On podstupi Betuliju,
10 odvrati vodu kâ u grad teciše, zdence pridgradske čini čuvati. Akiora, vojvodu svoga od Amoniti, jer reče da neće moći Židove svojevati ako ne budu zgrišili Bogu svomu, vezana čini popeljati i pridati Betulijanom, obitući se zajedno s
15 njimi ga zgubiti. Nesta vode u gradu, htihu se pridati. Ozija, knez od grada, moli jih da bi još čekali pet dan pomoći božje. Judita, udovica sveta i plemenita, kara jih da bihu Bogu roke postavili. Sama onuj noć moli se Bogu, ureši se,
20 pojde s rabom svojom Abrom ka Olofernu i nakon četvartoga dne, kad on pijan zaspa, otkla mu glavu nožem njegovim, stavi ju na grad, vojske se pristrašiše, grajane jih tiraše, biše, odriše, bogati se vratiše. To videći Akior, prija viru njih
25 i pribiva s njimi u Betuliju. Od Jerosolime dojde veli pop Eliakim sa svimi popi Juditu viditi: Boga slaviše, nju hvališe. Ona svojimi pojde u Jero-

# THE HISTORY IN BRIEF
## WHICH IS CONTAINED IN THESE BOOKS

Nabuchodonosor, the King of Babylonia and Assyria, reigning at that time in the City of Ninevah, did defeat Arphaxad, the King of the Medes, near the River Euphrates. He sent to his neighbours that they should submit to him: they did not want to submit. He sent his commander Holofernes off with his army: where e'er he went, he did conquer. At length he came to the land of Israel. There was great fear throughout the land. In Jerusalem many prostrations and sacrifices were made as offerings to God. He approached Bethulia, turned away the water that flowed into the city, and placed a guard upon the wells beneath the city walls. Achior, his commander of the Amonites, who did say that Holofernes would not conquer the Children of Israel unless they sinned against their God, he had bound and delivered unto the Bethulians, swearing to slay him together with them. The water in the city finished, they wanted to surrender. Ozias, ruler of the city, entreated them to wait five days more for God's help. Judith, a saintly and noble widow, reproached them for that they had set a term for God. That very night she did pray to God, bedeck herself, and go with her servant Abra to Holofernes, and at the end of the fourth day, when he fell drunk asleep, she cut off his head with his own knife, and place it on the city wall; the troops were terrified, the city dwellers drove them off, beat them, triumphed over them and returned wealthy. Seeing that, Achior accepted their faith and dwelt with them in Bethulia. From Jerusalem came the high priest Joakim with the elders to see Judith: they glorified God and praised her. She went to her own people in Jerusalem;

solim; pokloniše se u tempal, dare prikazaše, i tuj se tri misece veselivši, domom se varnuše.
30 Judita posli parvoga muža Manasesa drugoga ne poja; živi sto i pet lit, leže u grob muža svoga; sedam dan ju puk sitova. Za nje života ne oćutiše nevolje rati nike: dan dobitja nje svako godišće bi baržen i čtovan od svega puka izrael-
35 skoga, dokla tarpiše u stan'ju svomu. Na svem vazda Bogu hvala. Amen.

made obeisance in the temple, offered gifts, and, having rejoiced there three months, did return home. After her first husband, Manasses, Judith took not a second; she lived one hundred and five years, and lay down in the grave of her husband; seven days did the people mourn her. During her lifetime the tumults of war were not felt: the day of her victory was each year hallowed and honoured by all the people of Israel, for as long as they abode in their homeland. In all things may God be praised for ever. Amen.

## ĆA SE U KOM LIBRU UZDARŽI

*Parvo libro.* Nabukodonosor dobivši Arfaksata, posla Oloferna s vojskom primati daržave, hoteći da gospoduje svim svitom.

*Drugo libro.* Kuda Olofernes projde s vojskom; kih poda se podbi; pride u Gabu; bi strah u Jerosolim; pozlobiše Akiora veziri, jer istinu govori od naroda jerosolimskoga.

*Treto libro.* Olofornes Akiora vezana zagna u Betuliju, hoteći ga zajedno s grajani pogubiti kad jih prime. Ozija zva Akiora i popove na večeru. Olofernes podsede Betuliju; bi u grad žaja, do pet dan se hotihu pridati. Judita jih kara.

*Četvarto libro.* Judita s Abrom pojde van grada; Bog joj prida liposti, budi da vele lipa biše; Olofernes, vidiv ju, za njom se zamami.

*Peto libro.* Olofernes dvor svoj i Juditu zva na večeru; pijan zaspa. Koliko je zlo žartje i opitje. Judita Olofernu otkla glavu i na grad postavi. Akior se obrati na viru i pribiva u Betuliju.

*Sesto libro.* Betulijani izidoše s oružjem. Vojske, vidiv Oloferna ubijena, jaše bižati; oni jih tiraše, i s dobitjem se varnuše. Eliakim, pop veli, s popi pride vidit Juditu; ona svojimi pojde u Jerosolim; u tempal se poklonivši, s vesel'jem se varnu. Živi lit sto i pet; puk ju sedam dan plaka; dan dobitja čtovaše. Amen.

# WHAT IS CONTAINED IN EACH BOOK

Book One. Nabuchodonosor, having conquered Arphaxad, sendeth Holofernes to take the lands with his army, desiring thus to rule the whole world.

Book Two. Where Holofernes passeth with his army; whom he conquereth; he cometh to Gaba; there is fear in Jerusalem; the advisors despise Achior, for he telleth the truth concerning the people of Jerusalem.

Book Three. Holofernes driveth the bound Achior into Bethulia, desiring to slay him together with the town's people when he conquereth them. Ozias summoneth Achior and the elders to supper. Holofernes layeth siege to Bethulia; there is thirst in the town, they wish to surrender by the fifth day. Judith reproacheth them.

Book Four. Judith and Abra go out of the city; God addeth to her beauty, though she is very beautiful; Holofernes, seeing her, is entranced by her.

Book Five. Holofernes calleth his court and Judith to supper; he falleth drunk asleep. On the great wickedness of gluttony and drunkeness. Judith cutteth off Holofernes' head and placeth it on the city wall. Achior converteth to the faith and dwelleth in Bethulia.

Book Six. The Bethulians go out with arms. The troops, seeing Holofernes dead, begin to flee; the Bethulians drive them away, and return with booty. Joakim, the high priest, cometh with the elders to see Judith; she goeth to her own people in Jerusalem; having made obeisance in the temple, she returneth with joy. She liveth one hundred and five years; the people mourn her seven days; they honour the day of her victory. Amen.

KNJIGE
MARKA MARULIĆA SPLIĆANINA
U KIH SE UZDARŽI

## ISTORIJA OD SVETE JUDITE

U ŠEST LIBRI RAZDILJENA
NA SLAVU BOŽJU POČINJU

### LIBRO PARVO

*Dike ter hvaljen'ja presvetoj Juditi,*
   *Smina nje stvoren'ja hoću govoriti;*
*Zato ću moliti, Bože, tvoju svitlost,*
   *Ne htij mi kratiti u tom punu milost.*
5  *Ti s' on ki da kripost svakomu dilu nje*
   *I nje kipu lipost s počten'jem čistinje;*
*Ti poni sad mene tako jur napravi,*
   *Jazik da pomene ča misal pripravi.*
*Udahni duh pravi u mni ljubav tvoja,*
10  *Da sobom ne travi veće pamet moja,*
   *Bludeći ozoja s družbom starih poet,*
   *Boge čtova koja, kimi svit biše spet;*
*Da ti s' nadasve svet, istini Bože moj,*
   *Ti daješ slatko pet, vernim si ti pokoj,*
15  *A ne skup trikrat troj divička okola,*

---

11. **Poet:** poete se zovu ki pišu verse *(Ovu kao i daljnje, istovrsne tiskane napomene napisao je autor.)*
15. **Trikrat troj:** devet biše božic i meju njimi Apolo s kitarom, kih poeti prizivahu na pomoć gatan'ja ali kantan'ja njih veras.

*Here Begin to the Glory of God*
*The Folios of Marko Marulić of Split,*
*In Which is Contained*
*The History of the Blessed Judith,*
*Divided into Six Books*

## *Book The First*

The glories and praises of blessed Judith
Shall I sing, and her bold deeds.
Confer on me, O God, I pray, Thy grace,
Nor lessen in me the measure of Thy mercy.
For it is Thou who didst give power to her labour,                     5
And beauty to her body, as well as purest chastity;
Now help Thou me,
So that my tongue may proclaim what my thought
   hath prepared.
May Thy love inspire in me a right spirit,
So that my mind may no longer wander                                   10
In the misguided company of the poets of yore,[1]
Who honoured gods which did constrain this world;
For Thou art holy over all, O God of Truth;
T'is Thou givest rise to sweet song, and peace to the faithful,
Not the thrice-three choirs of maids,[2]                               15

---

1. Poets: Poets are they who write verses. (Marulić explains the word "poet," which evidently he felt to be unfamiliar in his dialect at that time–HC.)
2. Thrice-three: Nine in number were the gods and among them Apollo with his lute, whom the poets envoked for aid whilst prophesying or performing their verse.

            *Pridavši još u broj s kitarom Apola.*
        Uzdvigni odzdola glas moj k nebu gori,
            Gdi tvoga pristola čtuju svetih zbori,
            Da der u tvem dvori bude ti uslišan,
20       Dokol izgovori od Judite pisan,
        Grad veli Egbatan sazida i sredi
            Kralj hvale pohvatan, Arfaksat od Medi;
            Pokol jur pogledi, da vlada narodom,
            Preza svoje zledi kih podbi pod sobom,
25      Mnjaše da ni robom, ni moćju od ljudi,
            Ni plemenitim rodom na svit mu para ni;
            Da pozna po sebi, jer slava človika
            Najveća, kâ se di, ne tarpi dovika.
        Da kakono rika barzo mimo hodi,
30       Tako svaka dika s vrimenom odhodi;
            I ki se uzvodi u višu oholast,
            Teže mu se zgodi kad pade u propast.
        Ki poni toku vlast i silu imiše,
            Zgubi svoj glas i čast kada ga razbiše;
35      I ki ga dobiše, jure potomtoga,
            Jer se oholiše, izgubiše mnoga.
        *Pored da je Boga, Nabukodonosor*
            Mnjaše se dilj toga — nimaše bo razbor —
            Jer skupiv mnogi zbor i polag Eufrata
40       Razvivši svoj šator, pobi Arfaksata.
        S vesel'jem u vrata ninivska ulize
            Goneći na jata sužnje u želize;
            Malo jih ubiže, mnogo jih zagubi,
            Napuni sve hiže blaga kô urubi.
45      Viteze poljubi, svakoga darova,
            Od koga nahoj bî, hrabro da se arva;
            Paka barune zva, ter sede mev njimi,
            Otvoriv usta svâ, govori prid svimi:
        *»Ja vami hrabrimi sve sebi podložih*
50         »Ča godir očimi mojima obazrih;
           »Slavan se učinih ter čtovan visoko,

---

   27. Slava segasvitnja.
   49. Govori Nabukodonosor barunom svojim.

Nor Apollo on the lute in their number.
Elevate from here below my voice to the heavens,
Where choirs of holy ones glorify Thy throne,
That only by Thee may it be heard,
As it poureth forth the song of Judith.  20

Glory-seeking Arphaxad, who did reign o'er the Medes,
Built round Ecbatane great walls of hewn stone,
For he saw himself a ruler of the nations,
Which he conquered without mercy,
And thought himself without equal in this world,  25
In slaves, and power, and nobility of birth;
Yet knew he in himself that human glory,[3]
And all that it might mean, lasteth not for ever.
For just as the river swiftly floweth,
So passeth all glory with time.  30
And he who boasteth himself greatly,
Shall fall the more surely into the abyss.
He who thus hath such power and might,
Loseth his fame and honour in defeat,
And they who defeat him, ruin him the more,  35
And have boasted themselves even higher.

Nabuchodonosor, thinking himself equal to God,
–For he lacked measure and reason–
Gathered a great multitude and on the Euphrates,
Having struck his tents, did smite Arphaxad.  40
To the gates of Ninevah returned he then in joy,
Driving before him flocks of slaves in chains;
Few of them escaped, many did he slay,
And filled he his houses with booty he had stolen,
Rewarded he his warriors, gave he gifts  45
To those who had bravely fought.
Then he called his officers and nobles, and did sit
In their midst and out of his own mouth said:[4]

"I through you, my brave ones, have subdued
All that my eyes have surveyed;  50
I have glorified and honoured myself,

---

3. The glory of this world.
4. Nabuchodonosor speaketh to his captains.

»*I glas dȉli mojih prostri se široko.*
»*Sada jure, poko nitkore ne stoji*
   »*U zemaljski oko ki me se ne boji,*
55   »*Poslat ću da koji s nami mejaš ima,*
   »*Zapovidi moji podložan prijima.*«
Ugodno bî svima, svi ga pohvališe,
   Razum, moć s ričima do neba uzniše;
   Posle odpraviše ki naglo hodeći
60   Mejaše objizdiše, gradove proseći,
Zapovid noseći Nabuk'donosora,
   Gospodstvo hoteći vekšega prostora.
   Ni gradi, ni hora, ne pokloniše se,
   I s tim, kad bi zora, k kralju vratiše se.
65 On tomu čude se, pomuča nikoko,
   A paka sarde se, ja pritit žestoko,
   Govoreći tako: da će svih zgubiti
   Ki ne htiše, kako on reče, učiniti.
   I priča vapiti: »Poznati ćeš ča sam —
70   »Toj će harlo biti — Karmele i Libam,
   »Cedar, pridavši k vam Damask s Cilicijom,
   »I svu riku Jordan sa svom Galilejom;
   »Jošće s Samarijom jerosolimski stan
   »I s Etiopijom dobro će biti znan,
75   »Ča more doma i van oblast i jakost mâ,
   »I koli sam silan s mojom daržavom ja.«
Zatim nimalo sta, priseže pristol'jem,
   Kô se sve zlatom sja ter dragim kamen'jem
   I svakim zlamen'jem kraljevske razblude,
80   Da to s ispunjen'jem skoro, skoro bude. —
O koliko blude ki kâ su došasna,
   Brez razbora sude kakono iza sna;
   Človik bo to ne zna ako ne očituje
   Njemu ki svaka zna i svud gospoduje.
85 Kralj tako jiduje — sunce svitla lica,
   Na zapad minuje, za more skri nica;
   Noć jure potica da narod, živine,

---

87. Učini se noć.

And word of my deeds reacheth far and wide.
And now that there be none
Who faileth here on earth to fear me,
I command that all who neighbour on our realm,    55
Obediently accept that which I command."

All were pleased and did laud him,
His wisdom, power they praised to heaven on high,
And messengers they sent who, hastening thither,
Crossed borders, traversed cities,    60
Bearing the command of Nabuchodonosor,
Who sought dominion over yet a greater realm.
But cities and lands did not submit to him,
And when it was dawn, the heralds returned to the king.
Astounded, he kept silence for a while,    65
Then, waxing wroth, he set to cruel threats,
Speaking thus: that he would slay all
Who would not do what he willed.
And he began to shout: "Thou shalt know what I am,
And that quite soon, O Carmel and Lebanon,    70
Cedar, and thereunto Damascus with Cilicia.
The entire Jordan River with the Galilee,
The City of Jerusalem together with Samaria,
And even Ethiopia, to them it shall be made known
What my might can do at home and abroad,    75
And what power my realm and I do possess."

Then without further ado, he sware by his throne,
Which glittered with gold and costly stones,
And by all the signs of his kingdom's pomp,
That this would soon, so soon come to pass.    80

O how they err who would speak of the future,
They reason without sense, as though they dream;
For man knoweth nothing if He hath not shown it
Who knoweth all and directeth all.

So the king rageth–whilst the sun's burning visage    85
Declineth in the west, and hideth prone beyond the sea;
Night hasteneth on, and the multitudes and beasts,[5]

---

5. It becometh night.

        Človik, zvir i ptica, pustiv teg, počine.
        Sam ov do istine, pripun rogobore,
90      Ležeć na perine, usnuti ne more.
        Ojme moj nebore! Gospodstvo ča t' prudi?
        Ne bdi sad nitkore; tebe misal trudi.
        Kakono kad bludi sobom simo, tamo,
        Bisan pas mev ljudi, pojti ne umi kamo,
95      Ner se varti samo ter ujisti preži,
        Onamo, ovamo, ciri se i reži:
        Tako t' ov, ki leži, misleći, sasvima
        Ništare ne teži, a pokoja nima;
        Glavom svuda kima i sobom privraća,
100     Posažmi očima da san se odvraća;
        Jere se navraća pečal kâ ga karti,
        Ter skupost pribaća sve hteći odarti:
        Sve joj daj požarti ča želi od svita,
        Li neće do smarti nigdare bit sita.
105     Još iz dna izvita ne biše sva zora,
        Ni rosa sa cvita opala, da gora
        Biljaše jur zgora visoko varhami,
        A struja od mora mišaše iskrami;
        Jure noć s tminami doli pošla biše,
110     Da još dan s zrakami uzišal ne biše,
        Kada se skupiše vićnici u komori,
        Jer jih kralj zoviše, kîm tako govori:
        »U svem mojem dvori sluge najverniji,
        »I va svakom zbori u svem razumniji,
115     »I meni miliji! Znajte da misal mâ
        »Vele me grize i ji dokla ne vidim ja
        »Da svaka mista, kâ na svit gospoduju,
        »Podložna budu i da svi mene uščtuju;
        »Zato odlučuju sa svimi imit rat
120     »Ki se ne obituju poda mnom da će stat.
        »A parvo ću obujat daržave od onih

---

93. Prilika.
103. Skupost nigdar sita.
105. Jâ zabiljivati zora.
113. Kralj skupiv viće govori.

Man, animal and bird, set aside their tasks and rest.
Only he, still full of bluster,
Cannot fall asleep as he lieth on his couch.  90

O thou poor wretch! What availeth thee lordship?
Now that none watch with thee, and thy thoughts
    torment thee?
How like the mad dog, dashing hither-thither,[6]
In amongst the crowds, and knowing not whither,
Turning and lunging and threatening to bite,  95
Backwards and forwards, snarling and growling:
So too he lieth and pondereth, and even though
He do nothing, peace he cannot find;
He tosseth his head about, turneth this way and that
Presseth his eyes shut, but sleep will not come.  100
For a tormenting sorrow doth pay him visits,
While a greed hungering for all things doth him prick.
Let it swallow everything in the world,[7]
Yet till it die it will never be filled.

From the abyss the dawn had not yet reddened fully,[8]  105
Nor the dew yet fallen from the flower, though the peaks
Of the mountain were starting to glisten,
And the currents of the sea to cast sparks;
The night was already betaking itself to the shades,
Though the day star had not yet raised its rays,  110
When the king's counsellors gathered in his chamber,
For he had summoned them, and addressed he them thus:[9]

"In all my court my most faithful servants,
And in every counsel wisest in all things,
And dearest to me, know that my thoughts do  115
Torment and consume me till the time I might see
All places that hold sway on the earth
Submit to me, and all people honour me;
Therefore I declare war on all those
Who do not swear to be under me.  120
First of all I will conquer the lands of those

---

6. A comparison.
7. Greed is never sated.
8. Dawn beginneth to break.
9. The king, having gathered his council, speaketh.

»Ki se ne htiše dat kakono ja hotih,
»Nere rugo i smih u takovoj stvari
»Činiše od mojih oni poklisari.« —
125 Slišavši to stari vitezi uistinu,
Kako kîm se mari vuhlit gospodinu,
Svaki svû kapinu sa glave snimiše,
Ter pad na kolinu, dvorno zahvališe:
»Hvala tebi«, riše, »kraljeva svitlosti,
130 »Da smo od najviše pri tebi milosti;
»A tvojoj jakosti jur se pristoji svom
»Prez svake pakosti obladati zemljom.
»Jer ki toko sobom grad more tvard biti,
»Ki ti s tvojom vojskom nećeš razoriti?
135 »Tko li će se mniti silan zadovolje,
»Ki će s tobom smiti arvat se na polje?
»Sada tvoje volje stvoriti odluku,
»Kako ti znaš bolje, u tvoju je ruku;
»Drago će bit puku, vesel će bit rusag,
140 »Kad tebe uzvuku na svega svita sag.
»Zatim će te tvoj trag vazda blagoslovit,
»Da rodivši se nag, tobom oblada svit;
»A glas će tvoj živit, svuda slavan hode,
»Dokol budu svitit zvizde, teći vode.«
145 Tom hvalom ushode, kralj veće uzbuja,
Kako kad se svode vali gdi je struja;
Ter hlepeć na tuja lovišća vrić mriže,
Kako ljuta guja gori glavu dviže.
»Ki stojite niže, moga slugu verna,«
150 Sad reče, »najbarže zovite Oloferna!«
Kad dojde: »Biserna kruna mi s',« reče, »bil,
»Strila zlatoperna, kud si god hodil.
»Hrabro si se nosil u sve boje tvoje,
»Tiral si jal ubil protivnike moje;
155 »A sada ovo je stvar kû ti ja velim:
»Skup ljudi, tokoje sve ča je tribi njim.
»Obrativ putem tim, ka zapadu poji,

---

129. Odgovor vićnikov.
151. Kralj govori Olofernu.

Who have refused to obey me as I required,
But subjected those envoys of mine
To scorn and derision in this matter."

Having heard this, his old warriors in truth,     125
Like them who would readily flatter their lord,
Tore, to a man, the hats from their heads
And, kneeling before him, curried him with praise:[10]

"Glory to thee," said they, "royal effulgence,
For that thou bestowest upon us thy most gracious favour;     130
And it doth indeed befit thy might,
Brooking no vile checks, to rule the whole earth.
For which city, on its own, might so gird itself about
That thou with thine army couldst not level it?
Who thinketh himself sufficiently powerful     135
That he might dare to confront thee on the field of battle?
Now decide as thou wilt,
As thou knowest best, t'is in thy hand;
Happy the people, joyous shall be the land,
When thou art established as ruler of all the world.     140
Then shall thy descendents alway bless thee,
For though they were born naked, through thee they
   rule the world:
And thy fame shall live, marching gloriously everywhere,
As long as the stars shine and the waters flow."

Exalted by this praise, the king swelleth even further,     145
As when waves rise in the face of strong currents;
And lusting to cast his nets in others' waters,
He reareth high his head, like a poisonous serpent.

"Ye who are my subjects," saith he, "call now
Holofernes, my faithful servant!"     150
When he came, said the king:[11] "Thou hast been
   my pearly crown,
My arrow of gilded feathers, where e'er thou hast gone!
Bravely hast thou behaved in all of thy battles,
Chasing, beating, slaying mine enemies;
And now, behold the matter I command thee:     155
Gather thy men and all that they would need.
Go forth from my presence against the west country,

---
10. The advisors respond.
11. The king speaketh to Holofernes.

»Grade ter župe prim i čin da su moji,
»Da me se svak boji, svaki da me čtuje,
160 »Kako se dostoji, gdi godi me čuje.« —
On o tom duguje po kraljevskoj župi,
Hoteć da vojskuje, junake sakupi;
Kad zbroji zastupi, piših jih biše tad,
S kimi se uputi, sto dvadeset hiljad.
165 Mladi bihu, prez brad, jakosti najbolje,
Arvati svaki grad pripravni dovolje,
Ali se na polje biti, protežući
Lukove bivolje, mačima sikući.
Još kino sidući na konjih vojuju,
170 Dvanadest tisući biše jih po broju;
Ustežući voju, jedino jizjahu,
Pripravni ka boju; konji jim arzahu,
Bistro se metahu igraje nogami,
Nozdarvi harkahu, mašući glavami;
175 A oni strilami bihu opasani
Ter britci sabljami po svīti pisani;
Gredihu šarani, kako premaliti
Siroke tarzani gdi su svaki cviti;
Na glavi priviti plavi tere beli
180 I perja naditi stojahu faćeli.
Sćitke obiseli, kopja uzvartahu;
Svi bihu veseli, talambas tučahu;
Niki privartahu garlom začinjući,
Niki popijahu kundir naginjući.
185 Prid njimi jizdući vojvode s tumbatom,
Na njih se obzirući uzmitahu batom;
Oružjem ter zlatom svaki se svitljaše,
Pera jim za vratom vitar zavijaše.
Prid svakim jahaše oprovda u krunicu,
190 Pod krunom imaše na uho barnjicu,
Zlat sćit i sulicu njegovu noseći,
Na njoj korugvicu, bedeva vodeći.

---

164. Hiljad je tisuća; biše piših sto i dvadeset tisuć konjikov dvanadeste tisuć.

Conquer cities and countries in my name,
So that everyone fear me and honour me,
As it befitteth, where e'er they might hear of me."  160

At that Holofernes ranged the king's lands:
Desirous of conquest, he mustered his brave men;
When he counted the troops, there were as he set out,
Of foot soldiers an hundred and twenty thousand.[12]
Youths they were, bare chinned, at the peak of their
   strength, 165
Ready and able to destroy any city,
Or fight hand-to-hand, drawing bison bows,
Slashing with their swords.
And of those who fight on horseback
There were twelve thousand in number.  170
Pulling up their reins, they rode all as one,
Ready for battle; and their steeds whinnied to them,
Prancing and dancing on nimble legs,
Snorting their nostrils and shaking their heads,
And the horsemen were girded about with their bows,  175
And keen swords, in festive attire.
They rode gayly clad, as when in the spring
The greensward is covered with all sorts of flowers;
On their heads were wound cloth hats,
Blue and white, adorned with feathers.  180
They showed their shields, brandished their spears,
All were rejoicing to the sound of the drums;
Some sang at the top of their lungs,
Others leaning back drank from a jug.
Before them rode their captains, adorned with turbans,  185
Wielding staffs of office, they inspected their men;
Each one shone with arms and gold,
And the wind whipped the plumes round their necks.
Before each went an equerry sporting a wreath,
'Neath which hung a ring at his ear,  190
And he bore his lord's shield and a pole,
On it a banner, and behind him followed his mare.

---

12. "Hiljad" is a thousand; there were of footsoldiers one hundred and twenty thousand, of horseman twelve thousand. (Apparently the numeral *hiljada,* which is common in the Serbian variant of Serbo-Croatian, and not unknown in the Croatian variant, where the term *tisuća* is however still prefered, as in Marulić's day, required an explanation for Marulić's readers–HC.)

   Tako ti hodeći varvljahu šerezi,
    Okolo jizdeći asirski hercezi,
195 Bani tere knezi visoka plemena,
    Sluge ter vitezi počtena imena.
   Svega naparćena tuj kola škripahu,
    Tuj noseć brimena kamil'je stupahu;
   Tuj voli kasahu, tuj bravi potiču,
200 Pastiri zviždahu za njimi i viču.
   Ni šibi, ni biču ne daju pokoja,
    Goneći optiču, biše t' jim do znoja;
   Mnoga bo ozoja ondi bihu tada,
    Kîm ne biše broja, kola tere stada.
205 Za svom vojskom zada grediše Oloferne,
    Ki svimi oblada s junake nesmerne.
   Svi sluge preverne okol njega bihu,
    Luk, strile operne u ruci jimihu;
   A druzi gredihu mašući praćami,
210 Kamen'je berihu u krilo rukami;
   Druzi šćipačami bihu se zavargli,
    A druzi sabljami kê bihu potargli.
   Suknje bihu svargli, župe pripasali;
    Rukavce uzvargli, bičve podpasali;
215 Barže t' bi ticali skačući, dubravom,
    Ner kad bi bigali jelini prid lavom.
   Njih ti s bedar stranom kolesa šćićahu,
    Kâ grede ravninom konji potezahu;
   Sprid i zad jahahu vitezi železni,
220 Kopja jim se sjahu i meči bodežni.
   Jaki da utežni pod njimi pastusi,
    Pojt u boj ušežni veće ner u gusi;
   Uza nje konjusi sve piši potiču,
    Ter od cvitja busi za klobuk zatiču.
225 Nici prîd potiču, a nici skut prime
    Uz konj se pomiču daržeć se za strime.
   A tuj ti mev svime, posridi okola,
    Ki biše nad svime, sijaše na kola,

---

205. Zastava Oloferna s svojim taborom.

And so the teeming armies went,
Round about them rode the lords of Assyria,
Governors and princes of high estate,                   195
Servants and knights of good repute.
Loaded with all manner of things, their carts creaked.
Their camels, bearing their burdens, moved on;
Oxen went at a trot, rams scurried,
The shepherds whistled and shouted at them.             200
Nor gave they their staffs or whips a rest,
They drove and ran and goaded till they bathed in sweat;
For there was then a great multitude,
Without number of carts and flocks.
And behind the whole army rode Holofernes,[13]          205
Who issued orders to his gaudy heroes.
All his most faithful servants did surround him,
Holding bow and feathery arrows in their hands;
And others rode swinging their slings,
And collecting stones in their laps by hand.            210
Others rode out with lances in their grasp,
While still others with the swords they had drawn.
They had stripped off their garments, girded their shirts,
Rolled back their sleeves, laced up their boots.
Swifter did they dash through the oak grove on their mounts,   215
Than deer fleeing before a lion.
On one side they were screened by the carts
Which the horses were pulling along flat ground;
Before and behind rode knights clad in armour;
Their spears and keen swords shone in the light.        220
'Neath them, strong but burdened, their steeds,
More eager for the fray than for plunder;
Alongside the equerries ran to keep up,
Snatching up sprays of flowers to put in their hats.
Some raced on ahead, others tucking up their long hems,   225
Moved along with the horses as they held on to the stirrups;
And here amidst them all, in the very center of the camp,
Was he who was above all, seated on a carriage

---

13. Holofernes' army with its camp.

    Kâ zgora i zdola sva bihu gvozdena,
230  A s varha do pola po gvozdu zlaćena;
    Kon njega usajena korugva ćuhtaše
    Bila ter čarljena, s daleč se vijaše.
  A on ti sijaše oholo, visoko,
    A sam pogledaše po vojsku široko;
235  Karvavo mu oko, čarljen biše obraz,
    Brada jur nikoko prosida, debel haz.
  Poćaše se i u mraz, toko biše pritil,
    Vas obal kako praz ki još ni strižem bil;
    A biše se povil svionim skenderom
240  I gojtane pustil, kićene biserom.
  Šapka staše s perom na glavi, doli pak
    Na bedrih sa srebrom sablja tere bičak,
    Gledaše ti ga svak; lipo ga odivaše
    Dolama ke utak zlatom prosivaše.
245  Oko njega staše dvakrat treti vezir,
    Mev njimi subaše, na svakomu pancir;
    Stahu kakono mir ki šćiti kaštila,
    Da u nj ne skoči zvir, ni protivna sila.
  Toj kolo pritila živina vuciše,
250  Uz kû druga čila naizmin grediše;
    Taj ti črida biše od jakih bivoli,
    Vranih konji liše ter čarljenih voli.
  Zadaka za koli gredihu farizi,
    A na njih do toli pokrovci grimizi,
255  Uzde zlati frizi, zlaćena žvaoca,
    Pisana po brizi zlatom sedaoca;
  Od zlata staoca sa strimi zlaćeni,
    Od hitra tkaoca popruzi šareni;
    A konji mašćeni po rep i po grivi,
260  Samo tud čarljeni, inuda svi sivi.
  Ne bihu predljivi, da bistra pogleda,
    Ne bihu sklitivi, da glumna ujeda,
    Motahu t' ureda skakćući nogami,

---

235. Kakov biše Oloferne.
245. Šest veziri i tokoj subaše staše oko njega na kolo.
253. Olofernji povodnici.

Which top and bottom was made all of iron,
And gilded over from front to back.                    230
Next to him fluttered a banner,
White and crimson, it waved from afar.
And he sat in arrogance, on high,
And glanced at his troops far and wide;
Bloody was his eye, ruddy his visage,[14]              235
Grizzled his chin and fat was his belly.
He sweated even in a chill, so gross was he.
Rounded as a ram before it is shorn;
He had wrapped himself about with a silk girdle,
And piping decorated in pearl.                         240
A hat of feathers lay on his head, down below
On his hip a sword sheathed in silver and a dirk,
And all stared at him; his tunic fit him well,
Its fabric shot through with gold.
Near him stood twice three viziers,[15]                245
Midst them lieutenants, in armor bedecked;
They stood like a wall that protecteth a castle,
So that no beast or fiendish power might gain entry.
Hefty animals pulled that carriage,
Along side them, as robust, walked others to relieve them;  250
And this whole herd was composed of mighty bison,
Jet black horses as well as ruddy oxen.
Behind the carriage came geldings,[16]
Crimson covered them to the ground,
Their reins had golden designs, their bits were gilt,  255
And their saddles scrupulously dappled with gold;
Straps of gold with gilded stirrups,
Colourful yokes woven by a master;
And the horses, with dyed tails and manes,
Here they are red, there all in gray.                  260
They were not skittish, but clear of eye,
Not spiritless, but playfully nipping,
They would twist about stamping their hooves,

---

14. How Holofernes did appear.
15. Six viziers and also lieutenants stood round about him.
16. Holofernes' parade horses.

          *Plešući poreda, zavarg se glavami.*
265   *Plaho ti bedrami pojdihu svartaje,*
          *Razmašuć parsami, stegna podžimaje;*
          *Svim se pojimaje, rekal bi lećahu,*
          *Tla ne doticaje, tako se dvizahu.*
          *A na njih sijahu lovci ter ptičari,*
270   *Na ruci jim stahu sokoli mitari;*
          *Harti ter ogari za njimi tičući,*
          *Kakono vahtari laptahu sačući.*
          *Prid kolom bijući bubnjahu nakari,*
          *Trumbite trubljući svirahu pifari,*
275   *A niki u citari zvoneći pojaše,*
          *Kralji ter cesari hrabrost počitaše.*
          *Tuj se razligaše sve polje s gorami,*
          *Rekal bi se oraše nebo sa zvizdami:*
          *S tacimi bukami levite dojdoše,*
280   *Kadno miri sami hjerički padoše.*
          *Tacih uspregnuše kon Sinajske gore,*
          *Kojino pojdoše Boga čut govore,*
          *Kad nitkor ne more prez straha čekati,*
          *Grom s trubljom sa gore kad priča praskati.*
285   *Da tko spovidati sva more čudesa? —*
          *Od konjske bahati zemlja se potresa,*
          *Ništar ne poresa, ni trava ni žito,*
          *Kuda vojska plesa, po sve ono lito.*
          *Tad lačan korito prasac ostavljaše,*
290   *Zvire strahljivito bigat ne umijaše;*
          *Na zemlji padaše ptica sa visine,*
          *Kad zavapijaše vojska iz dubine.*
          *Od praha magline dvizahu se gori,*
          *Kakono oblačine kad marče po gori,*

---

277. Prilika. Josue s vapajim i s trumbitami leviti obajde grad Hjeriko, i miri od grada sami padoše.

284. Prilika. Mojses govoreći na gori s Bogom, puk se pristraši i odstupi od gore, čuvši trublje i glas strašan božji.

291. Gdi je velika množ, kad zavapije, ptice, kê nad njimi uzlete, padu, jer se rastupi ajer ter se ne moć budu uzdaržati.

Prancing against one another and tossing their heads.
They moved coyly, shaking their shanks,                     265
Expanding their chests, pressing their flanks;
Breasting everything, it seemed they were flying,
Neither touched they the ground, so lept they above it.
On them rode hunters and fowlers,
On whose arms stood falcons in molt;                        270
Whippets and hunting hounds raced after them,
Like guards hot on a trail.
Before the carriage cymbals were struck,
Trumpets trumped, pipes piped,
Whilst others, picking the lute, did sing,                  275
And praised the bravery of kings and emperors.
Here did the whole field and the mountains resound,[17]
One would say, the whole firmament was coursed through.
With such a noise did the Levites arrive
To knock down the walls of Jericho.                         280
At such a noise did those at Sinai
Leap, when they heard God in speech,
When none could tarry without fear,
As thunder did peal and trumpet from the mount.[18]
But who then can relate all those wonders?                  285
The earth doth shake from the horses' hooves,
Nothing groweth, neither grass nor grain,
Where e'er the army rangeth all that summer.
E'en the enhungered pig leaveth the trough,
And the frightened beast knoweth not to flee.               290
Birds fall to the ground from on high[19]
When e'er the army letteth loose with a shout.
Dust storms arose to the heights,
Like unto cloud banks that darken the hills;

---

17. A comparison. Joshua with a shout and the Levites with their trumpets did go 'round the City of Jericho, and the walls of the city fell of themselves.
18. A comparison. Whilst Moses spake on the mount with God, the people grew afraid and stepped away from the mountain, for they heard trumpeting and the terrible voice of God.
19. When there is a great flock and it beginneth to screach, the birds that fly above it fall, for the air gapeth open and they cannot sustain themselves on it.

295   Seli tere dvori, poljem kada gode,
    U dne al u zori, paljihu se hode.
  Nestaniše t' vode gdino postojahu,
    Zato vred na prode prit se popeljahu;
    A kad se brodahu, sklopiv moste nike,
300   Deset dan s'brojahu brodeć se prik rike.
  Tej sile tolike puni bihu luzi,
    Kakono njive ke pokriliše pruzi,
    Kad egipski muži s kraljem ki biše kriv,
    Ostaše u tuzi, osmi bič oćutiv.
305   Tko je toliko smiv ki bi jih dočekal?
    Al nadaleč vidiv da se ne bi pripal? -
    Mnju ti bi uzdarhtal despot, car i sultan,
    Tere bi pleća dal, meč ne podarvši van,
Nit bi se oziral bižeći noć i dan.

---

302. **Prilika.** Pruzi su kobilice kê pokriše polje od Egipta, ne hteći Faraun pustiti puk božji. I toj bi osmi bič, jer parvo toga dao jim biše Bog inih nevolj kih bi u vseje deset.

Villages and farms, at dawn or at dusk, 295
Were torched where they went, every time.
And where e'er they stopped did the waters dry up,
So to find streams they went on.
And when they took count to ford a river,
Ten days did it take to number the throng. 300
The woodlands were filled with such a force,
Like the fields that were covered with locusts,[20]
When the Egyptians and their pharaoh, who had erred,
Did grieve, as the eighth plague they witnessed.
Who might be so bold as to await them? 305
Or, seeing them from afar, might not faint?
I think e'en a despot or emperor or sultan
Would shudder and run, without drawing his sword,
Nor would he look back, but run night and day.

---

20. A comparison. Locusts are grasshoppers which did cover the fields of Egypt, pharaoh not wishing to let the people of God go. And that was the eighth plague, for before that had God given them other misfortunes, of which there were in all nine.

## LIBRO DRUGO

    S tom vojskom prejakom Oloferne greduć,
       Asirijom jur svom prošal biše hituć,
       I sve svaršiti vruć — da mu ne bude ukor —
       Ča veli kralj moguć Nabukodonosor.
5   Nigdir nimav opor, dojde na livi kraj
       Cilicije, do gor angiskih, ter ondaj
       Obhode kako zmaj, popali posade
       I sva mista onaj zauja i grade.
    Da jer se ne dade poglavit grad Melot,
10     Odarvat se nade, zaskoči mu oplot;
       Tud'je u jedan bot vaze ga, potuče
       Svih u njem, kako skot, a njega rastuče.
    Ča zasta, razvuče i pošadši varsi,
       Poplini i svuče ki bihu u Tarsi;
15     Još da se ne omarsi, kon zemlje Celine
       Potar pak i smarsi izmaelske sine.
    Prik Eufrata mine, vodeć Asiriju,
       Posede konfine, Mesopotamiju;
       Kaštile parćiju vaze, polja, gore,
20     I ki su u Siriju grade ter njih hore
    Kê zahitit more, od Mambre potoka
       Dokla plâčē more sa strane istoka;
       Pak počan od boka Cilicije, dokom
       Jafeta široka mejaš takneš nogom.
25  Madijane sobom povede zarobiv,
       Njih blago s živinom prez izma porobiv,
       A svih onih pobiv ki s meči i s bati
       Jaše mu stat protiv, ne hteć se pridati.
    Damasku prid vrati prišad, malo potarp,
30     Poče žita žgati kâ jur prošahu sarp;
       Zaćarni kako čarp polje, kad požar sta,

## Book The Second

Holofernes, riding with his arrogant army,
In haste had traversed all Assyria,
Desirous to accomplish all–lest he be reproached–
Which mighty King Nabuchodonosor had commanded.
Finding resistance nowhere, he had arrived 5
At the mountains of Ange, to the south of Cilicia,
And there, ranging like a serpent, did burn their farms,
And occupy all their cities and fortresses.
But the powerful city of Merloth would not surrender,
They hoped to repel him, but he lept o'er their parapets, 10
Took them forthwith at one blow, slaughtered
Them all like cattle, and leveled the town.
What remained he tore to bits, and, passing o'er the peaks,
He captured and enslaved all who were in Tarsus;
Nor yet tasting of any food, he shattered the land of the
  Chellians, 15
And scattered the sons of Ishmael.
Having crossed all Assyria, he passed beyond the Euphrates,
Took possession of its confines and Mesopotamia;
He took the lands of the high cities, and fields and hills,
And the fortresses of Syria, and all the territories 20
Which he could compass, from the stream of Arbonai
Till he came to the sea from the east;
Then set he out from the flanks of Cilicia
Till he touched his foot to the borders of Japheth.
He led with him the sons of Madian, 25
Despoiled all their goods and their flocks, nor missed any,
And smote all who with sword or mace did think
To resist him, not wanting to surrender.
Arriving before the gate of Damascus, he tarried,
Set ablaze the grain that awaited the harvest. 30
When the fire ceased, the field was black as burnished tile,

   Ne bi utlin ni karp, da golo sve osta.
 Jer hip još ne posta, posiče i drivje,
   Ni loza ne osta, u zemlji ni žil'je;
35 Umri svako smin'je, svak sebi strah ima
   Videć da sapin'je nad glavom je svima.
 Kako kad tmastima kreljutmi oblak gust
   Prikriv nebo dima, miga, gromi u hust,
   Mornar jidra popust, upije ter hiti,
40  Da k kraju svarnuv šust u porat uhiti;
 Težak darhće liti, boji se, govori:
   »Grâd mi će pobiti vinograd i bori,
   »I žita kâ gori jur podivaju klas.
   »Ojme! Zgubih skori mû hranu, moj trud vas!
45 Tako t' ognjenu vlas Oloferna slišav,
   Trepi svak ter za glas pitav i sva kušav,
   Posle poslaše, i stav oni tiho prida nj,
   Ništare ne postav, pridaše se poda nj.
 Jer bit ne moguć sa nj, pridat se voliše,
50  I spustivši se na nj, komu tako riše:
   »Ne htij od nas više, molimo, sila tvâ,
   »Oer kâ naša biše tvâ da je zemlja sva.
 »Bolje je da se dâ u službu svaki živ,
   »Ner da svak biži tja, al umre duh pustiv;
55  »Odvrati poni gnjiv, tebi će čast biti,
   »Milost nam tuj stvoriv, kralj će t' zahvaliti.
 »Jerbo će voliti mista da mu služe;
   »Puna po sve liti, ner pusta da tuže;
   »Dostojni su uze i smarti, bud takoj,
60  »Kino se ogluše dat se sili jakoj.
 »Da evo sve ovoj, ča je u našoj nadi,
   »U ruci je tvojoj, župe, sela, gradi,
   »Polja ter livadi i stada živine:
   »Budi ta sva sadi kraljeve svitline.

---

  37. Prilika. Kad je zal oblak i fortuna, mornar se boji na moru, a težak na polju, svaki se zlu nadijući: tako se svi jaše bojati videći fortunu sile Olofernje.
  50. Tako govore, jer se bojahu da jih ne pobije pridavši se.

No place to hide, not a shred was left, all was bare.
Then waiting no more, he cut down their trees,
Not a vine remained, nor a root in the ground;
All boldness did vanish, each fearing for himself  35
Seeing that doom hung o'er all their heads,
As when on darkling wings thick clouds[1]
Cover the sky, whistle, flash, rumble in a pile,
The sailor, lowering his sails, howleth and scurrieth,
Returneth to land to clutch the port's ropes;  40
The fieldhand trembleth in summer, in fear he saith:
Hail will pound my vines and furrows,
And the grain whereon the head already heaveth into sight,
Woe! In one blow I have lost my food, all my labour:
And so too they who hear of Holofernes' fiery might,  45
Each quaketh, beggeth news; and, when all hath been tried,
Sendeth envoys to stand humbly before him,
And, asking nothing in return, submitteth to him.
For, as none might make himself his equal, they prefer
To surrender and so speak with him thus[2]:  50

"Seek no more from us, we pray, O Mighty Power,
Than that the land which was ours now be thine.
For it is better that each become a servant,
Than that all flee from here or loosing their spirit perish;
Turn away thy wrath, therefore, to thee will be all honour,  55
Do us this kindness, and the king will thank thee.
For he prefereth cities that serve him,
Filled the year round, than deserted ones that mourn.
Worthy are they of bonds and, yea, e'en death,
Who are deaf to the call to submit to thy might.  60
Be that as it may, here lieth all for which we hope
In thy hand: districts, villages, fortresses,
Fields and glades and herds of cattle:
Be this now all to thy royal eminence.

---

1. A comparison. When the cloud is wicked and there is a storm, the sailor on the sea feareth, and the peasant in the field, each expecting evil: in this way did all begin to fear as they saw the storm of Holofernes' might.
2. Thus they speak for they feared he would slay them if they surrendered.

65 »Blago svake cine i sva obitil s njim,
　　»I sve stvari ine, i mi sami zatim
　　»Služit ćemo sasvim kraljevu velikost,
　　»Listo nas ti sad prim u miru na milost.«
　　Bi miran i usilost ne dâ jim za sada,
70　　Ner da ne bude prost nitkore od tada
　　Zakona ki kralj dâ, i kad godi čuje
　　Ime kralja, tada poniknuv da čtuje.
　　Oholosti luje vidi li ovoga,
　　　Ki se ne sviduje, mneć se vekši Boga?
75　　Malo potomtoga umrit će, smardit pak,
　　Ter ostaviv mnoga, s najmanjšim bit jednak.
　　Koga sad trepi svak, nitkor ga hajat neć',
　　Kad u grob nauznak prostre se jur ležeć;
　　I ki je sad hoteć da vlada zemljom svom,
80　　Malo, malo posteć, plća će bit čarvom.
　　Ki sada svakim zlom pritiska narod ov,
　　Pritisnut će potom njega kamen zakrov;
　　To t' će biti njegov konac, ki sad stoji
　　Ter mni da je takov da ga se i smart boji.
85 Da ovi li koji daje se oholosti,
　　Kâ se ne pristoji, još nima milosti:
　　Uze blaga dosti, i talić zauja,
　　Ni još jim ne prosti, vojnikov priuja.
　　Svak skuta poduja, čtujući človika,
90　　Tolik strah obuja mista svakolika;
　　Gospoda velika od gradov pram njemu
　　Gredihu, razlika vesel'ja čine mu.
　　Svitilnike žge mu, krune donošahu,
　　Pojahu jošće mu ter tance vojahu;
95　　Tuj ti mu zvonjahu gusle s leutaši,
　　Dipli privartahu, s njimi nakaraši.
　　Ni tim ne zaparši on tvardosti svoje,
　　　Mnozim grad potarši, posiče i hvoje,

---

72. Hotiše da adoravaju Nabukodonosora kako boga. Protiv toj oholiji ovdi pisac govori.

98. Pod hvojami koga godi stabla velika boge svoje čtovahu.

Goods of any price and our entire households too,    65
And all other things, and we thereunto,
Shall serve completely thy royal majesty,
Only receive us now mercifully in peace."

He was content, and used no force for now against them,
But so that none of them might be henceforth free    70
From the king's law, he commanded when they hear
The king's name, that they bow down and honour it.³
Hath one ever seen arrogance like unto his,
Who hath no perception, but thinketh himself greater
    than God?
A bit later, and he shall die and then stink,    75
And having left behind many things, will be made equal
    to the least.
Him whom all now fear none will then regard
As he lieth stretched out on his back in the grave;
And he who is desirous to rule the whole world,
Tarry but a bit, and he will be food for the worms.    80
He who now presseth the peoples with all manner of evil
Himself shall be pressed by a stoney blanket.
Such shall be the end of him who now standeth
And thinketh he be such that e'en death doth fear him.
But he who giveth himself to an arrogance    85
That is not meet, hath no pity in him:
Having taken many goods, and of captives not a few
Whom he releaseth not, he enslaveth warriors too.
Each maketh obeisance, raising his hem to reverence,
Such terror overtaketh the cities roundabout;    90
Mighty lords from their castles made their way
To him, bringing him various entertainments.
They lit candles before him, offered him crowns,
They even sang and danced in his presence;
Their lute-players strummed for him,    95
They piped on their flutes, and drummers did drum.
Nor at that did he soften his mercilessness,
For he leveled many a castle, and hewed down

---

3. He desired that they adore Nabuchodonosor as a god. Here speaketh the writer against such arrogance.

    Gdi bozi njih stoje: »Bog«, reče, »ni nitkor,
100  Ner koga se boje, Nabukodonosor.«
    Dili se od tih gor, sobalsku Siriju
     Projde shodeć niz gor i još Apamiju,
    Mesopotamiju projde tokoj, ter tu
     Dopri Idumiju gdino palme restu.
105  Gabalsko jest u tu daržavu vladan'je,
     Grade prija sve tu i sve njih iman'je;
    Tuj sidi, sabran'je sve vojske čineći,
     I tuj u to stan'je trideset dan stići.
    Dokla dohodeći svi se dosabraše.
110  Misec jur sviteći drugoč se kazaše;
     Tankorog hojaše, kakovno biše bil,
    Kada tuj pristaše parva čela svih sil.
    Ne bi tko bi se ril; ki su to slišali,
     Strah jih je svih ubil, svi su se pripali;
115  Jesu se bojali Židove da i njim
     Rasap ter pečali ne budu kako inim;
    Da grad Jerosolim, Oloferne došad,
     Nastupom oholim ne stare. Zato tad
    Slaše ljudi ki šad Samarijom uzgor
120  Der gdi je Hjerik grad, sedoše navarh gor.
    Još da niki opor bude, opletoše
     Sela tere njih dvor, i koko mogoše,
    U gradu snesoše žita za potribu
     U toj vrime loše čekaje pogibu.
125  Upisavši knjigu pop veli Eliakim,
     Jer imiše brigu, posla tad k onim svim,
    Ki su u Dotaim i kon Esdroloma,
     I nakon njih inim: da ne side doma,
    Ner da bljudu droma i klance zaskoče,
130  I gdi je proloma, da zavale ploče,
     Jeda s' ne proskoče protivnici naprid
    Hteći da rastoče jerosolimski zid.
    Ne bi t' jih strah ni stid, sve toj učiniše,

---

109. Misec dan sta totu, dokla se zbere vojska.
116. Jaše se bojati Židove.
129. Drom ali drum zove se put općeni.

The groves of their gods.[4] "God," saith he, "is none
But he whom they fear, Nabuchodonosor." 100

He departed from those mountains, went down
Through Syria Sobal and Apamia too,
Crossing also Mesopotamia, he reached
Idumaea, where the palm trees grow.
This is the realm of Geba, 105
And he took their fortified places and all that they owned;
And he pitched camp, gathered in all his troops,
And tarried there thirty days with them.
Till all came together and gathered,[5]
The shining moon had shone itself a second time; 110
It rose as a sliver, as it had been
When the first troop of his army had arrived.
Nor was there one to resist; whoever heard them
Was seized with fear, did writhe in terror.

And the children of Israel were also frightened 115
That them, like the others, ruin and misery would strike[6];
Lest Holofernes, when he came before Jerusalem,
Obliterate it in arrogant attack. So they sent
Men out who, mounting through Samaria,
Near to Jericho, occupied the hill tops, 120
To offer some resistance, and they fortified
The towns and their homes, and as best they could,
Carried into the cities victuals for their needs,
Awaiting in those evil times their certain death.
Also the high priest Joakim penned a missive, 125
For he was burdened by care, and sent it to all
Who lived in Dothaim and in Esdraelon,
And after them, to others: that they not tarry at home,
But watch the highways[7] and occupy the steep places,
That where there be a passage, they rain down stones, 130
That the enemy might not break through
To demolish, as he wished, the walls of Jerusalem.
They had no fear or shame, and did all

---

4. 'Neath the groves of any large tree did they worship their gods.
5. It was a month till the army gathered together.
6. The Jews began to take fright.
7. "Highway" is a public road. (Marulić is explaining his use of the word "drom" [which he also renders as "drum"] to his readers–HC.)

<pre>
        Ča jim pop svet i sid pišući veliše;
135     U gradu vapiše s moljen'jem prihilim,
        Ter se ponižiše svi postom nejilim.
     Popove još zatim pleća svâ odiše
        Vrićišćem tim oštrim ter suze roniše,
        Dičicu prostriše prama templu božjem,
140     A oltar pokriše zgora cilicijem.
     Tad svi jednim vapjem moljahu govore:
        »Bože, koga u svem kripost svaka more,
        »Pozri nas odzgore i glase naše čuj,
        »Ter, ki nas sad more, strahov nas obaruj.
145  »Ti ne daj da ovuj pogibil prime puk,
        »Puk ovi tvoj, kojuj dat misli ljuti vuk;
        »Jakost od tvojih ruk oblomi ovoga
        »Oružje, strile, luk, ki ne čtuje Boga.
     »A ne daj da tvoga grada stan primisti,
150     »I templa ovoga oltar onečisti;
        »Svagdan se na nj misti za slavu tvoju tov
        »Žartja kôno čisti grišnike od grihov.
     »Vidiš li kako ov po svitu tekući,
        »Lovi karvavi lov, derući, koljući,
155     »I grade orući? Ti Jerosolime
        »Ubran, čuvajući da ju ne obime
     »Ni mista nje prime, ni blaga njeje, kô
        »Ne dvi, ni tri zime kupismo, da lit sto
        »I još desetkrat tô, od kô ti tuj stavi
160     »Puk ovi, ni tad gô kad Egipat ostavi.
     »Ne daj da se izbavi milih sinak mati,
        »Ter se ne zadavi, ne moguć gledati
        »Gdino jih vezati svih budu žestoko,
        »I bijuć peljati u ropstvo daleko.
</pre>

---

135. Bogu se jaše priporučati.
138. Cilici harvacki se zove vrićišće.
141. Molitva puka jerosolimskoga.
152. Žartja: sacrificia.
160. Jer zajamši u susid sude i pratež diliše se od Egipta po riči božjoj, ki je voljan jednomu vazeti, a drugomu dati, kakono koga je sve ča je gdi.

That the holy and aged priest in his letter had commanded;
In the city they cried out in prayer earnestly,[8]     135
And they humbled themselves with rigid fasting.
And the priests clothed their shoulders
In scratching sackcloth and shed copious tears.[9]
They placed their children before the temple of God
And clothed the high altar in sackcloth.     140
And all prayed with one cry, saying:[10]

"O God, whose power is over all,
Look upon us from above and hear our supplications,
And deliver us from the fear of those who would now
   slay us.
Let not the people suffer the destruction–     145
This people is Thine– which the ravening wolf doth intend
   them!
May the power of Thine hands shatter
The arms, arrows, bows of him who doth not fear God.
Let him not displace the sanctuary of Thy city,
Nor profane the altar of this temple,     150
On which daily to Thy glory are placed
The choice parts of the sacrifices[11] which cleanse sinners
   of their sins.
Dost Thou see how he roameth through the world,
Hunting bloody prey, rending and piercing
And leveling cities? Protect Thou now     155
Jerusalem, lest they come to besiege it,
Or conquer its environs, and all its goods which
Not in two or three winters, but for a hundred years
   we have gathered,
And ten times more, since Thou didst settle
This people here, who was not naked even as it left Egypt.[12] 160
Let not the mother be shorn of her dear sons,
Nor be crushed, unable to watch,
When they are all cruelly bound
And, beaten, led off into distant captivity.

---

8. They began to entreat God.
9. In Croatian sackcloth is called "vrićišće." (Marulić explains the Croatian calque of Latin "cilicium"–HC.)
10. The prayer of the people of Jerusalem.
11. Sacrifice: sacrificia. (Marulić is explaining Croatian "žartja" with the Latin word–HC.)
12. For having taken their neighbours' vessels and goods, they departed from Egypt according to God's word, Who freely taketh from one and giveth another, to Whom all things belong where e'er they might be.

165 »Nemilostiv toko on jest da grad vazam,
　　　»Svih ključi nizoko, ne prašća ni ženam,
　　　»Da svakim vašćinam za rugo prida jih,
　　　»Gdino gleda sajam, gdi vide muži njih.
　　»Ti stegni moć ovih ki svojom žestinom
170　　»Nadhode lavov svih svě sile jačinom;
　　　»Ako im ti tvojom vlastju neć' zabranit,
　　　»Tko je tâ ki sobom more se obranit?
　　»Ti nas poni shranit dostojaj se, Bože,
　　　»Njih tuj ne ustanit; kripost tvâ sve može;
175　　»Tebi se podlože molimo u suzah,
　　　»Ne daj da nas slože u tolicih tugah.
　　»Od meči, od uzah, kad si godi hotil,
　　　»I od jacih rukah ti nas si slobodil;
　　　»Ti nas jesi vodil prik mora po prahu,
180　　»Onih si potopil kino nas tirahu.
　　»Po tvom jošće strahu, kako obita sam,
　　　»Kino ovde stahu, ustupiše se nam;
　　　»Pogledaj poni k nam, Gospodine, sada,
　　　»Milost tvu pošlji nam, kakono i tada.
185 »Ufan'je i nada naša sam jesi ti,
　　　»Ti ne daj da vlada nami ki s tobom ni.
　　　»Grišni smo, Bože, mi, da milost tvâ gdi je?
　　　»Puk tvoj ni p'je ni ji, »pomiluj!« upije.
　　»Pomiluj, tebi je dostojno stvoriti
190　　»Milost onim ki je budu ti prositi;
　　　»Mi ćemo t' služiti i dušom i udi,
　　　»Zakon opslužiti, pomoć naša budi.« —
　　Tako t' ovi ljudi vikahu plačući
　　　U takovom trudi li Boga zovući;
195　　Eliakim tišući njih, reče: »Dim vam ja,
　　　»Da Bog vas slišući imit će smiljen'ja.
　　»Poste ter moljen'ja listo ne pustite,
　　　»Dilo poniženj'ja svagdan prikažite;
　　　»Nu se spomenite od Mojsesa, vam dim,
200　　»Tere dobro vijte koga dobi i čim.

So merciless is he that, when he take a town,     165
He casteth all beneath his feet, showeth mercy not
   even to women,
But giveth them over to loathsome acts for their disgrace,
As the people looketh on, as their husbands watch.
Rein Thou in the power of them whose cruelty
Exceedeth e'en the lions in the strength of their might.     170
If Thou wilt not inhibit them with Thy power,
Then who is he who alone can protect himself?
Deign, thus, O Lord, to protect us,
Nor strengthen them: Thy power can do all things;
Falling before Thee, we pray Thee tearfully,     175
Let us not be cast into so many miseries.
When e'er Thou didst desire it, from swords and bonds
And powerful hands didst Thou liberate us.
Thou didst lead us through the sea on dry land,
And didst drown those who pursued us.     180
Then too, for fear of Thee, as Thou Thyself didst promise,
They who dwelt in this land made way for us.
Look now, O Lord, upon us,
Send us now Thy mercy as then Thou didst send it.
Our hope and trust Thou art alone,     185
And let not him rule us who is not with Thee.
We are indeed sinners, Lord, but where is Thy mercy?
Thy people neither drink nor eat, but cry "Have mercy!"
Have mercy, it is meet that Thou shouldst confer
Mercy upon those who pray Thee for it;     190
We shall serve Thee both in soul and bodily parts,
And fulfill Thy law: be Thou our help."

So the people shouted crying,
In such distress calling to God;
Joakim did console them, saying: "I tell you     195
That God will have mercy and hear you.
Only do not neglect the fasting or the prayers,
Display each day the work of humility;
But remember Moses, I say to you,
And perceive well whom he conquered and how.     200

»Pride u Rafadim Amalek kralj, hotuć
»Da s božjim pukom svim boj bije, uzdajuć
»Da je vele moguć oružjem i mnoštvom
»Ter da će svih potuć došad na mistu tom.
205 »Ne mečem ni šćitom Mojses dobi njega,
»Da molitve hitom, i pobi ga svega:
»Tako će i sega zločinca pobiti
»Bog vaš, ako njega budete moliti.«
Pričaše postiti, te riči slišeći,
210 I žartja činiti, udilje moleći,
Vrićišća noseći, po glavi luženi,
Da budu proseći Bogom pohojeni.
Kada ču ognjeni Oloferne taj glas,
Da su zasedeni puti od gorskih staz,
215 I da židovska vlas pripravno čeka boj,
Čudi se i starši vȁs i gnjivan bi zatoj;
I sazvav u dvor svoj amonske vojvode,
»Tko su«, reče, »ovoj ki po varsih hode'
»Bljudući prohode? Kȉ gradi? Kȃ hitrost?
220 »Mnogi li se plode, mnoga li njih jakost,
»Da imiju sminost stati protiv naju?
»Ali našu hrabrost ni sile ne znaju?
»Sami nas ne haju, toliko su smini,
»Ter nas ne sritaju s častju kako ini.«
225 To rekši, zapini usta, zube sharsti,
A njim ti namini zala svake varsti;
Splete parste s parsti, a glavom pokima,
I od toke garsti zavrati očima.
Svaki jih strah ima gledat ga u lica,
230 Gdi marmnje mev njima, ter obrazom nica
Stahu, kako dica kad skulan dȋ: »quitto«,

---

201. Ovo je bilo, kad gredihu od Egipta. Josue se s Amalekom bijaše, Mojses na goru moleći staše; kada dvigniše ruke, dobivaše puk njegov, a kad jih spušćaše, dobivahu neprijatelji. Jaše mu podaržati ruke ki s njim bihu, i tim dobiše Amaleka.
213. Oloferne se rasardi čuvši ali vidivši da se neće pridati strane izraelske.
231. Prilika.

King Amalek came to Rafadim wanting[13]
To do battle with all God's people, for he thought
Himself most mighty in arms and armies,
And that he would smite all when he arrived at that
   place.
Neither with the sword nor the shield did Moses
   defeat him,                                                          205
But with the blows of prayer did he conquer him.
So shall this enemy be conquered
By your God, if ye pray to Him."

They began to fast as they listened to these words
And to offer sacrifices, always in prayer,                              210
Wearing sackcloth, ashes on their foreheads,
Beseeching God that He visit them.

When fiery Holofernes heard the report[14]
That the passages of the hill country had been shut up
And that the children of Israel, prepared, awaited war,                 215
He was amazed, and uttered threats, and waxed wroth.
And calling to his court the captains of Ammon,
"Who are," said he, "these who, dwelling in the hill
   country,
Stand guard o'er the passes? What are their cities?
   What is their cunning?
How great are their multitudes, how mighty their power                  220
That they have the effrontery to stand against us?
Do they not know our bravery and our might?
They pay us no attention, so brazen are they,
And they meet us not with honours, as do the others!"
Having said this, he frothed at the lips, he ground
   his teeth,                                                           225
And he conjured evil of all kinds for them;
He twisted his fingers, tossed back his head,
And in his loathing rolled round his eyes.
Each of them feareth to look him in the face
As he rambleth before them; down cast they                              230
Their gaze, like children when the tutor saith: "Silence!"[15]

---

13. This was at the time they left Egypt. Joshua contended with Amalek, whilst Moses stood in prayer on the mountain; when he raised his arms, his people prevailed, and when he lowered them, the foe prevailed. They who were with him began to uphold his arms, and thus was Amalek defeated.
14. Holofernes grew angry hearing this and seeing that the Israelites would not surrender.
15. A comparison. (Marulić uses *quitto* as the tutor's command–HC.)

        *Ter pojamši biča zakrikne sardito.*
        *Parva stanovito glava od Amoniti,*
        *Akior, uhilito poča govoriti:*
235    *»Htij se dostojiti slišat, gospodine,*
        *»Jer ću ti praviti od togaj istine.*
        *»Nî bo tribi hine da k tebi donesu,*
        *»Ni stvari kê ine, nego kêno jesu.*
        *»Puka strane te su, ki s zemlje kaldejske*
240    *»K zemljam pride kê su mesopotamejske.*
        *»Jer slave nebeske Boga sebi obraše,*
        *»Ostaviv boge kê oci njih čtovaše;*
        *»U Karah počaše tada pribivati,*
        *»Jednoga kad jaše Boga virovati.*
245    *»I pokol stiskati glad mnogi jâ vas svit,*
        *»Taj puk pojde stati, dvigši se, u Egipt;*
        *»Gdi sta četarsta lit i bi toko množan,*
        *»Da nitkore zbrojit njega ne bi možan.*
        *»Egipski premožan kralj nima jur mira,*
250    *»Da taj puk pobožan toko se rašira;*
        *»Ter ga tako stira rabotom parteći*
        *»Da on jur ponira od truda hodeći.*
        *»Zato se moleći vapiti k Bogu jâ,*
        *»Bog njega mileći, Egiptu rane da;*
255    *»Kada, da idu tja, Egipt jim dopusti,*
        *»Tad saržba božja sta, nevolja popusti.*
        *»Da jer se uzgrusti kralju od Egipta,*
        *»Na njih ti pripusti, li da jih pohita,*
        *»Pohitav uplita, koko bude moći,*
260    *»Trudom brez izvita, u dne ter u noći.*
        *»Tad Bog svoje moći skazav, ki bižahu,*
        *»Posla jim pomoći, jere se bojahu:*
        *»Nakraj mora stahu, more se rastupi,*
        *»Puk po suhu prahu naprida postupi.*
265    *»Za njimi pristupi kralj svimi silami,*
        *»More ga opstupi i pokri vodami;*
        *»Zamisi s kolami ljudi, konje, meče,*

---

235. Govoren'je Akiora, u kom skazuje Holofernu stvari puka izraelskoga.

And reaching for the whip, beginneth to shout angrily.

Without hesitation, the captain of the Ammonites,
Achior, humbly began to speak[16]:
"Deign hear me, my lord,                                                                     235
For I shall tell thee the truth of this matter.
For it is not meet that I bring lies before thee,
Nor report things other than as they are:
These districts are a people's who from Chaldean lands
Came to the lands that are Mesopotamia's.            240
For they chose for themselves the God of heavenly glory,
Having abandoned the gods that their fathers had revered;
They began then to sojourn in the land of Canaan,
When they first believed in the One God.
And when a famine oppressed the whole world,        245
That people moved itself down into the land of Egypt,
Where they remained four hundred years, and became
   so numerous
That none could count them all.
The mighty king of Egypt could no longer find rest,
For that pious nation increased so;                             250
And he brought them low, and broke them with labour,
That they stumbled in fatigue as they walked.
Then in prayer they began to cry out to their God.
God, in that He loved them, smote Egypt with wounds.
When Egypt allowed them to part from there,         255
God's wrath did abate, and the plague subsided.
But the king of Egypt did repent of his decision,
And loosed his troops upon them to retake them,
And having caught them, would have yoked them
   as he could
To their labours, without respite, night and day.         260
Then God, showing His power to those who fled,
Sent them His aid for they were sore afraid.
They came to the edge of the sea, the sea split,
And they moved ahead on dry ground.
After them in pursuit was the king with all his army,   265
The sea overwhelmed and covered him with its waters;
It tossed people with carriages, horses, swords,

---

16. Achior's speech, in which he relateth to Holofernes the matters of the people of Israel.

»Kopja s korugvami, nitkor ne uteče.
»A kad puk proteče kroz Čarljeno more,
270 »K pustinjam priteče od Sinajske gore:
»Voda kû ne more od gorčine piti,
»Slatka bî i more svak je se napiti.
»Četardeset liti s nebes jim dažji man,
»Kruh, kim se nasiti, beruć ga svaki dan;
275 »Na koju godi stran sobom obratiše,
»Sela grade i stan prez boja dobiše.
»Jere se arviše za nje vazdi Bog njih,
»Nigdar ne izgubiše, ner kad grih sape jih;
»Kad bo bogov tujih prijaše ostaviv
280 »Boga svoga, Bog svih podloži pod svoj gnjiv.
»Niki mart, niki živ u hlapstvo idiše,
»Niki sve izgubiv plačan ostaniše;
»Opet jih varniše Bog u parvoj stan'je,
»Kada jih vidiše čineći kajan'je.
285 »Po njega smiljen'je kralju Kananeju
»Daše raščinjen'je i još Jebuseju,
»I s njim Ferezeju, i Eteju toje.
»Eveju i Amoreju kraljem još tokoje.
»Sva mista njih koje godir gdi imihu,
290 »Učinivši svoje, u miru živihu;
»Dobrosrićni bihu vazda der do vika,
»Dokol ne padihu u prezpravdja nika.
»Nî jošće velika svitlost, ophode svit
»Vrimena selika, svaršila vele lit,
295 »Da je zaveden bit puk ovi i živil
»U strane tujih mist, jer biše sagrišil;
»Pak se je obratil k Bogu svom, i Bog njih
»Jest jih oslobodil od uze protivnih,
»I u mistih ovih, povarnuv se, leže,
300 »Ter u rukah svojih Jerosolim darže.
»Sada, ki teg teže, mili gospodine,
»Jeda jih grih steže, izuvij istine;
»Jer ako krivine kê jesu, dilja kih

---

293. Veliku svitlost zove sunce.

Spears with banners: not one escaped.
And when the people had passed over the Red Sea,
They came to the wastelands of Mount Sinai:  270
The water which for its bitterness could not be drunk
Was sweet, and each could drink his fill of it.
For forty years they received mana from the heavens,
The bread they filled themselves with as they gathered
   it each day;
Whichever direction they turned in,  275
They conquered villages, cities and homes without battle.
For their God did battle for them,
Nor did they ever lose, except when they did sin,
For when they took alien gods, abandoning
Their God, God put them down in His wrath.  280
Some died, others went into captivity;
Others, losing everything, remained to weep;
Once again God returned them to their former state
When He saw them truly repenting.
Through His mercy caused He the downfall  285
Of the king of Canaan, and the kings of the Jebusites,
And of the Perezites and Hetites,
And of the Hevites and the Amorites as well.
Having conquered their lands where e'er they went,
They made them their own, and lived in peace;  290
And they prospered always, for as long
As they did not fall into sin.
The great light[17], oftmany times
Circling the world, still had not completed many years,
When that people were carried away and lived  295
In the lands of alien cities, for they had sinned;
But then they returned to their God, and their God
Did free them from the fetters of their enemies,
And return them to their lands where they now live,
And they hold Jerusalem in their hands.  300
Now, kind lord, those who pull the plow,
If sin overtake them, recognize this truth;
If their errors are such

---

17. "The great light" is the sun.

»Bog se ne pomene da jur pomože njih,
305 »Pojdimo najti jih, komu su zgrišili,
   »Bog će pridati jih tud'je tvojoj sili;
   »Ako l' prevridili nisu svomu Bogu,
   »Moć sa hitri dili njih ti ne premogu.« —
Tako po razlogu besidi Akior,
310 Da razlog pod nogu postavi nerazbor;
Jer vidit bi ukor ovo vezirom svim,
Čude se da opor može tko biti njim;
I rasarjeni tim jaše mislit on čas,
Da ga obvargu zlim, da ga zgube danas.
315 »Tko je,« riše, »ov pas ki vo mni da neće
   »Puk oni, zgledav nas, obratiti pleće?
»I na gori steće da će osiditi,
   »Da će ne bižeće protivit nam smiti?
»Ki ni piš hoditi, ni na konju sidit,
320 »Ni se zna šćititi, ni meč u boj nosit!
»Pojmo jih zatirit ali jih poklati,
   »Ako se budu rit; tada će poznati
   »Ča se je rugati, hinbeni Akior,
   »Kad i njim metati budemo s ovih gor.
325 »I vås židovski dvor vidit će da je bog
   »Nabukodonosor, ki je toliko mog,
   »A ne Gog ni Magog.« — Tako se sarjahu,
Tako žegući rog na njega marmnjahu.
Piše ti na prahu i po salbun sije,
330 Ki se oholu bahu svît dat usiluje;
Jer on ne slišuje nauk od istine,
Ki se uzvišuje u slavi tašćine,
Pravdu pogarjuje, ljubi vuhavšćine.

---

315. Pozlobiše Akiora ki pravo govoraše; da Bog ga ne ostavi, budi da i on biše poganin, tada vojvoda od Amoniti.

327. Gog, Magog: toj su imena židovska. Tako govore rugajući se.

329. Na prahu ča se upiše, smarsi se; a ča se po salbunu sije, ne nikne: tako je zamani dobar svit ki se daje oholim ki neće slišati, kako ovi ne slišaše Akiora.

That their God no longer thinketh to help them,
Let us go up against those who have sinned, 305
And God will place them straightway in thy power;
If they have not been iniquitous to their God,
Then neither force nor all manner of cunning will avail thee."

And so Achior spoke with great sense,
So that sense might put senselessness beneath it. 310
But all this seemed to the viziers like a reprimand:
They wondered if someone would oppose him.
And they were angered, and thought at that moment
To accuse him and slay him that very day.
"Who is," they said, "this pup who thinketh[18] 315
That that people, espying us, will not turn and run?
And that standing on their mountains, they will hold out,
Or dare to oppose us and not flee?
A people who knoweth neither to march or ride;
Nor how to hold a shield, nor bear a sword in battle! 320
Let us root them up, or cut them down
If they resist us; then shall deceitful Achior
Understand what it meaneth to scoff,
When we throw him too from the peaks of these
    mountains.
And all the children of Israel will see 325
That God is Nabuchodonosor, the mighty,
And not Gog or Magog."[19] And so they raged,
And goaded him foully and murmered against him.
He writeth in the dust and soweth in the sand[20]
Who would try to advise the bold blusterer. 330
For such doth not harken to true knowledge
Who exalteth himself in vainglory,
Scorneth truth, and loveth flattery.

---

18. They were angered against Achior who spake the truth; but God did not abandon him, though he was a pagan, the leader of the Amorites.
19. Gog, Magog: these are Jewish names. Thus they speak when they curse.
20. What is written in the dust is wiped away; and what is sown in the sand groweth not: thus is good counsel in vain which is given to the arrogant who will not hear it, as these did not hear Achior.

## LIBRO TRETO

  Da vazda pravednih Bog jest obaroval,
   I još po smarti njih vičnji njim život dal;
   Tako ti ni pušćal Akior da zgine,
   U nevoljah upal zacića istine.
5 Veziri toj čine', Oloferna gnjivu
    Pridaše vrućine, kako konju živu
    Kad teče po njivu kad mu dadu ostrog,
    Popostrese grivu tere poljuti nog;
  Priskoči plot i stog i potok prikine,
10   Koliko je uzmog, teče, vrata rine:
    Tako sobom hizne ovoga gardoba,
    Kad ju pouzdvigne vezirska hudoba.
  Poni u toj doba Oloferne sardit,
   Jer vlada njim zloba, tako jā govorit:
15 »Ki si prorok da rit umiš, Akiore,
  »Da narod taj oprit nam se sada more,
  »Uzdaje se u gore al u bogu nikom,
   »Da njima pomore? Hiniš nami u tom.
   »A sad da ti sobom iskusiš, jer nitkor
20 »Zvat se more bogom, ner Nabuk'donosor,
  »Kada mi vās njih zbor obratimo pod mač,
   »Zadit će naš kosor i tebe u rubo tač.
   »Ča blidiš, ali plač ča t' lica zaliva,
   »Ako tvoja pritač znaš da ni laživa?
25 »Živit ćeš gdi živa ostane njih dobar:
   »Gdi li ona saspiva, saspit ćeš i ti zgar;
   »A da t' bude ta stvar, vedte ga da side
   »U taj grad pod ki bar mā hoću da ide.
  »U ki kad unide tere zaskoči rov,

---

  6. Prilika.
  14. Govori Oloferne Akioru.

## Book The Third

But God hath always preserved the righteous,
And given them, after death, eternal life;
So He did not let Achior perish,
Who had fallen into misfortune for the truth's sake.
At the viziers' incitement, Holofernes' wrath               5
Grew greater still, as when a fiery steed,[1]
Racing o'er the field, is spurred on,
And he shaketh his mane and stampeth his hooves,
And leapeth hedge and rick, and stream doth broach,
With all his might he raceth, o'erturning the hurdles:      10
So doth Holofernes' rancour kick on its own,
Pricked on by the viziers' wickedness.
And at that time, he so enraged,
Seized with malice, spoke in this fashion[2]:

"What sort of prophet art thou, Achior, to say              15
That this nation might resist us,
Relying upon their hills or some god
To deliver them? Thou liest to us!
And now, so that thou thyself mayest learn that none
May be called god but Nabuchodonosor,                       20
When we put all their multitudes to the sword,
Our blade shall also pass through thy sides.
Why palest? Why bathest thou thy face in tears
If thou knowest thy tale is not false?
Thou shalt live whilst their power yet doth reign;          25
If it fail, so shalt thou too fail thereupon;
And so that this might happen, take him away
To that fortress against which I shall send my army.
And when he enter it and cross the trench,

---

1. A comparison.
2. Holofernes addresseth Achior.

30      »Činte da ne izide nitkore živ, ni ov.« —
        Grad biše ovi nov, na gori sijaše,
        Oko njega obrov, Betul'ja se zvaše.
     Grad taj uzdaržaše narod Simeona,
        I njemu služaše polja strana ona;
35      Tamo moć siona pogna Akiorom,
        Da smarti zakona tarpi s gradskim zborom.
     Dojdoše pod varhom, i tuj ga vezaše,
        Nazad ruku s rukom k stablu kô tuj staše;
     Jere im ne daše pojti priko meje,
40      Ki s gore metaše iz praće kamen'je.
     Oni ga ondeje vezana pustiše,
        Ovi zgor tudeje sašad, odrišiše
        I k gradu odniše. Pitaše grajani,
        Zač mu učiniše toj Asirijani?
45      Od Betulijani dva poglavitija
        Bihu tada zvani Karme ter Ozija:
        Prid njimi izvija sve ča mu se steče,
        Akior, da prija proplaka, pak reče:
     »Ovo se zareče Oloferne sardit,
50      »Da će sva na meče mesa vaša razdit,
        »I mene s vami ubit — nato me je zagnal;
        »Bog daj da bi ta prit njemu na glav upal.
     »Toj se je prisegal stvoriti vam sa mnom,
        »Jerbo sam ja rekal: Bog vlada zemljom tom,
55      »I Bog vaš sam sobom da ima moć i vlas,
        »U vrimenu ovom obarovati vas.« —
     Kad sliša puk taj glas, Bogu se pokloni,
        Smakši beritu s vlas i suzami roni,
        Moleći da ukloni njih od pogibili,
60      Kôm karvavac oni mnozih jur uhili.
     »Ti se,« riše, »smili, o Bože gospodstva,

---

32. Betulija, grad ki najpri podstupi došad u zemlju židovsku. Simon je bio jedan od sinov Jakoba koga kolino daržaše Betuliju.
42. Dovedoše Akiora u Betuliju.
49. Govoren'je Akiora Betulijanom.
61. Molitva Betulijani Bogu.

See to it none leave it alive, neither he."  30
This fortress was new, it lay atop a hill,
Around it entrenchments, its name Bethulia.[3]
The tribe of Simeon held it,
And those alien fields did serve him;
Thither did that mighty power drive Achior,  35
So that he suffer death with the people of that place.
They came to the foot of the hill and bound him,
Hands behind his back, to a tree that stood there;
From above men cast stones from their slings
So that those below might not cross o'er their border.  40
Then they left him bound there,
They from above, having descended, released him[4]
And led him to the fortress. The inhabitants did ask:
Why did the Assyrians do this to him?
Two captains of the Bethulians at that time  45
Were called Charmis and Ozias:
Before them did he lay out all that had transpired.
First he burst into tears, then said:[5]

"This did wrathful Holofernes swear:
To rend your flesh with his swords,  50
And to slay me with you–and then he drove me hither;
O Lord, may that threat fall back upon his head.
He swore to do these things to you and to me,
For I had said: God ruleth this earth,
And your God by Himself hath power and might  55
At this time to deliver you."

When the people heard these words, they bowed to God,
Tore the coverings from their heads and wept copious tears,
Praying that they be spared the destruction
With which that butcher had bereaved many another[6].  60
"Have mercy," they said, "upon us, O Lord God,

---

3. The city of Bethulia, which is encountered the first upon entering the land of Israel. Simon was one of the sons of Jacob whose generation did hold Bethulia.
4. They led Achior into Bethulia.
5. Achior's speech to the Bethulians.
6. The Bethulians pray to God.

»Pozriv naši dili ki su umiljenstva;
»I onih oholstva, ki prite, pogledaj,
»Rasap ter ubojstva odvrati i ne daj;
65 »Ukaži da si haj ufajućih u te,
»Ukaži da s' nehaj ufajućih u se.
»Smiri, molimo, nje ki se uznašaju
»Silom svojom a tvê jakosti ne znaju.
»Čuvaj, brani naju, jerebo si ti sam,
70 »Ki s' u gornjem raju slava ter dika nam.«
To rekši i suzam ustaviv izvora,
Pričaše obistram tišit Akiora,
Govore: »On zgora ki gleda, stvoritelj
»Od svakoga stvora bit će t' obaritelj
75 »I svih nas spasitelj tako da još onih
»Hoće bit raspitelj ki hlepe rasut svih.
»I kada nas od njih Gospodin slobodi,
»Dozov k tebi tvojih, ter stoj s nami ovdi;
»Toj ti budi godi', da ki je s nami Bog,
80 »I tebe pohodi, jer znaš da je svemog.«
Tuj Akior nebog zlovoljan stojaše,
Kakono niz oblog u zemlju gledaše,
Ter riči slišaše, jur tvarje daržeće
Da u kom ufaše, ostavit ga neće.
85 Jur sunce ničeće nagnul' biše kola,
Svitli obraz hteće zamaknuti dola;
Istočnoga okola jur šćićaše stranu
Noć, dvižuć odzdola čarnokosu glavu:
Kadano poznanu Akiora cilost
90 Na svom zazva stanu Ozijeva milost
Jer znaše da blagost velika jest tomu,
S ljubavlju prijat gost u koga je domu.
Sazva još k ovomu i pope za bratstvo,
Da žežinu svomu pokripe mlohavstvo;
95 Večeru i jistvo obilo napravi,

---

73. Tiše Akiora.
85. Jur bi večer, i tad Ozija zva Akiora i pope na večeru.
95. Uči se ovdi kako imaš gosta počtovati.

And behold the works of our humility,
As Thou lookest upon the pride of those who threaten us,
Ruin and robbery turn from us, permit them not;
Show that Thou carest for those who trust in Thee,     65
Show that Thou carest nought for those who trust in themselves.
Bring down, we pray, those who boast
Of their own might, and Thy power fail to recognize.
Keep and protect us, for it is Thou alone
Who in highest heaven art our glory and praise."     70

Having spoken thus, and stopped up the source of their tears,
They began from both sides to console Achior,
Saying:[7] "He Who gazeth from above, the Creator
Of every creature, will be thy protector
And saviour of us all, and at the same time     75
The destroyer of those who lust for our ruin.
And when the Lord doth free us of them,
Call thine own to thee and live here with us;
Know full well that He Who is our God,
Attendeth also to thee, for thou knowest He is omnipotent."     80
Wretched Achior gloomily did stand,
And as if through a window, stared into the ground,
But he listened to those words, and held all the more
That He in Whom he hoped would not abandon him.
The sun, going down, had taken to his carriage,[8]     85
Wishing to conceal his bright visage below;
Night was covering the eastern lands of earth,
As she raised from below her head of jet black;
When Achior in all his well-known honesty
Was invited home by Ozias in his well-known kindness,     90
For he knew that God doth love him
At whose house a guest is received in charity.
He summoned as well the priests to his table
So that they, weak from fasting, might restore themselves;
He set forth a dinner with abundant food,[9]     95

---

7. They calm Achior.
8. It was already evening, and at that time Ozias summoned Achior and the elders to supper.
9. Here is taught how one honoureth a guest.

              Za stolom toj ljudstvo više sebi stavi.
              Ništar ne ostavi ča se čtu pristoja,
                 Da veće ljubavi skazati nastoja;
                 Toj i ovoj poja, ne sebi hoteći,
100         Jer se ne dostoja, da druzih nudeći.
              Svi Boga hvaleći, Akiora nukaje,
                 Akiora tišeći, Akiora gledaje,
                 Li njega svidaje da se ne zlovolji,
                 U Bogu uzdaje, Bogu da se moli.
105        Sedeći za stoli, oni se čtovahu,
                 Ophode okoli sluge jim landahu;
                 A druzi služahu vino iz bokare,
                 Čarljeno livahu u zlate pehare.
              Ča peku, ča vare, druzi ti nošahu
110        Na čiste lopare: jedno donošahu,
                 Drugo odnošahu, svartaje nogami,
                 Dvorno pristupahu, segaje rukami.
              Visoko s svićami stahu kandeliri,
                 Mnogimi zrakami odsivahu miri;
115        Ne biše tko sviri, ni s bukom govori,
                 Ni smijeć se ciri, ni šale ki tvori.
              Svaki tiho zori ča oni pomina,
                 Ča ov odgovori, ča li sam namina,
                 Ona smartna tmina, kû na vratoh vide,
120        Od karvi, od plina, da k njim ne unide.
              Toj ovoj obide razlika besida,
                 Li na tom izide da grada i zida,
                 Ako Bog ne svida, na branicih vahtar
                 Zaman bdi i sida, a na vratih vratar.
125        Zastoj imiše mar, ustav se na nogu,
                 Da skupe puka bar u svû sinagogu,
                 Ter se mole Bogu — moliše ga svu noć,
                 U potribu mnogu da jim pošlje pomoć;
              Jer je zdravje i moć i utočišće njih,

---

115. Ne biše bo vrime toga.
123. Ps(alam): Nisi dominus custodierit civitatem, frustra vigilant, qui custodiunt eam.
125. Imiše mar: imiše pomnju.

And seated his guests e'en above himself.
Nor did he leave out ought that honour requireth,
So that he might show the greatest possible charity.
He took this and that, but never for himself,
For that was not meet, but offered it to others.              100
Praising God, pressing Achior to eat,
Comforting Achior, watching Achior,
They all took care lest he fall into despair,
And urged him to pray, trusting in God.
Seated at the table, they regaled one another,              105
Servants, circling round, waited on them;
Others served them wine from a pitcher,
Pouring crimson into golden goblets.
What was baked or boiled still others bore
On clean platters: one thing was brought,              110
Another taken away, servants spun on their feet,
And offered more with their hands, politely approaching.
High above were lamps with candles,
The walls reflected their many rays;
There was none to make music, none who spoke loudly,[10]   115
None who snickered as he laughed, none who made jokes.
Each carefully observed what the other said,
Or what this one did answer, or what he himself intended,
Lest that deathly darkness of blood and pillage
That stood beyond the door enter in upon them.              120
Their varied conversation touched upon this and that,
But it was clear that on the bulwarks of the fortress
And the wall, if God doth not keep them,[11]
The watchman watcheth in vain, and the porter at
    the gate.
And so they were disposed, rising to their feet,[12]       125
To gather the multitude of the people into their synagogue,
To pray to God—and they prayed all night long,
That in their great need He send them assistance,
For He is their health and their strength and the
    refuge of them

---

10. For this was not the time for that.
11. The psalm: Except the Lord keep the city, the watchman waketh but in vain. (Marulić cites the Latin text of Psalm 126: 1 of the Vulgate [127 of the KJV]–HC.)
12. "Were disposed": were minded. (Marulić explains the Croatian word "mar," care, disposition–HC.)

130 Upalih u nemoć dilj straha protivnih. —
Od postilj istočnih dviže glavu Titan,
Osini tmin noćnih da zarene hitan;
Jur svital biše dan, i vidiše sa gor,
Kîmno tuj biše, stan, vojske greduć uzgor;
135 Kako prisičen bor na zemlju padoše,
Na golu glavu zgor pepeo vargoše.
Moleći rekoše: »Bože pomiluj nas!
»Jer evo dojdoše poterti nas danas;
»Kako ti viš i znaš, skaži tvoje čudje,
140 »Da puka tvoga vlas ne pogine tudje.«
Vazeše orudje i stine u skuti,
Stupiše osudje gdi su tišnji puti,
Gdi su klanci kruti meju klesurami,
Da, stavši na ljuti, meću se praćami.
145 A vojske stranami varvljahu ka gradu,
Blizu pod stinami okolom da padu. —
Potok niz livadu marmnjući teciše,
Pod borjem u hladu, bistar i čist biše:
Grana ga grediše vojena po brigu,
150 Ter vode nesiše tad gradu posridu;
Ovu da pristrigu, Oloferne reče,
Tako da napridu ka gradu ne teče.
Da još nedaleče od grada stojahu
Poduboke bleče gdi vodu čripahu
155 Grajani ter p'jahu, skrovito pohvate',
Jere se bojahu da jih ne uhvate. —
Uz toj se navrate Amon i Madijan
Satoru prid vrate Olofernu izvan,
»Znaj«, riše, »da on stan ne uzda u ljude,
160 »Da u tuj gorsku stran na koj stražu bljude.
»Da ti poni bude taj prez arvanja grad,
»I grajan zloćude ne budu vridne sad,

---

131. Isteče sunce. Titan: to je ime sunca, kô je mnozimi imeni zvano od starih poet.
133. Ki na gori stražu činjahu, vidiše gredući vojske i jaše Boga moliti.
152. Oloferne odvrati vodu, Betulijanom; studence, ki bihu pod gradom, čini čuvati.

Who are helpless for fear of the enemy.            130
From his eastern posts Titan raiseth his head,[13]
And hasteneth to drive away the shades of night's darkness;
It was already bright day, when those camped on the
    mountain tops[14]
Perceived that armies were moving up toward them:
They fell to the ground like trees cut at the base,      135
And sprinkled ashes on their bare heads.
In fervent prayer they spoke: "God, have mercy!
For they have come to destroy us this day;
As only Thou canst, show us a miracle,
Lest the power of Thy people fail forthwith."        140
They took up arms and gathered stones in their sleeves,
And marched to where the passages are narrowest,
Where the slopes are steep between the canyons,
So that they might stand on the cliffs and shoot their
    slings.
But the armies swarmed up to the fortress from the
    flanks,                                                   145
To approach its walls they circled around.
Murmuring a brook flowed down through the meadow,
'Neath the wood, in the shade, it was clear and clean:
A branch of it had been channeled along the hill,
Which brought the waters to the middle of the city;    150
Holofernes ordered that it be diverted
So that it no longer flow to the fortress.[15]
Not far from the fortress there also were
Deep wells, whence the inhabitants drew water
And where they drank, dipping pails in secret,       155
For they feared they might be captured.
Thereupon Ammon and Moab went up
To the entrance of Holofernes' tent, who stood outside it.
"Know," they said, "that this fortress trusteth not in men
But in the mountain height on which they keep guard.   160
For this fortress to surrender to thee without resistance,
And that the wiles of its inhabitants cause us no harm,

---

13. The sun riseth. Titan: this is the name of the sun, which is called with many names by the ancient poets.
14. They who kept guard on the mountain saw the troops approaching and began to pray to God.
15. Holofernes turneth away the water of the Bethulians; he placeth a guard on the wells 'neath the city walls.

»Stav stražu, kâno pad kon zdenac, ne dade
»Vazimat vodu kad ki od njih napade.
165 »Tim ti se pridade vas puk on od volje,
»Ali se raspade od toke nevolje;
»Od tada jih kolje žaja kad ti veli
»Odvratit u polje njih potok on veli.«
Slišav on ča želi, naredi vojvode,
170 Kîm moćno zapeli da čuvaju vode.
I sunce odhode' dvadesetkrat pride,
Li oni ophode i na zdencih side.
Od tada unide u gradu sušina,
'Z gusteran izide jure i vlažina;
175 Od nikih dubina još vode imaše,
Kâ žmulom cidina mîrom se diljaše.
Ništar manje znaše svak da sva ne bi svim
Žeju, kâ jih žgaše, ugasila tad njim;
Stopit ust ne bi čim, prisihat jâ jazik,
180 Usne pucat, za tim bliditi vas človik.
Skupiv se puk velik, muži, žene, dica,
Tko star, tko mladolik, k Oziji se stica;
Svaki smina lica (sminost nevolja dav)
Njemu oporica i tuži, prida nj stav.
185 »Bog,« riše, »sud postav' mev tobom i nami,
»U kolik trud pridav varže nas u plami;
»Ne htij podvit rami da mirno govoriš
»Prî ner nas žajami nevoljno umoriš.
»Sad oto sâm vidiš, veće ne moremo
190 »Ov grad, u ki sidiš i ki u nj živemo;
»Sami sebe ćemo dat Asirijanom
»Prî nere budemo martvi sa svim stanom.
»Evo smo pod članom jur tvoga vrimena,
»Da želimo slanom polahčat brimena;
195 »Plače brižna žena i jure rada je,
»Da je povedena s dicom mruć od žaje.
»I svim nam laglja je od meča smart vidit,

---

173. Odkol izvan nimaše vode do dvadeset dan, jaše zlo stati žajom.
184. Tuže na Oziju da se ne hti do parve dati.

Place a guard at the well and let it not allow
Any who come for water to draw ought.
Thus will that entire people surrender of their own will.   165
Or they will perish in great misery;
For thirst hath plagued them since thou didst command
That their great stream be diverted into the field."
Having heard what he wanted, he sent out his captains
And ordered them sharply to guard the waters;   170
And the sun, going down, came up twenty times,
As they surrounded and did sit at the wells.
Thereupon a great dryness reigned in the city,[16]
From the cisterns the last moisture had disappeared;
At some great depths there was still water   175
Which they filtered and doled out by measure.
Nonetheless they knew it never would suffice
To slake the thirst that tormented them all.
There was nought to moisten their mouths, their tongues
   began to dry,
Their lips to crack, and the whole person to wax pale.   180
Then many of the people, men, women and children,
The old and the young, gathered to go before Ozias.
Each bravely (with the bravery misery doth give)
Addresseth him, lamenting, as they stand before him.[17]

"May God," they said, "judge between thee and us,   185
Causing us so much grief, he casteth us into the flames;
Do not lack the will to hold peaceful converse
Before thou slayest us miserably with thirst.
For now thou thyself seest, we can bear no more
In this city thou inhabitest and where we live;   190
We will surrender ourselves to the Assyrians
Before we and the whole city fall down dead.
For we are so oppressed by these times
That we would quench the burden of our thirst with salty
   water;
The care-laden woman lamenteth and is glad   195
If she and her children, dying of thirst, be enslaved.
And death by the sword seemeth easier to us all

---

16. Since they had no water from outside for twenty days, they began to suffer from thirst.
17. They complain against Ozias, who would not yield from the start.

»Ner se mučit zjaje', a nimat ča popit;
»Tad i uzu tarpit vele manji jest trud,
200 »A Boga u svem hvalit i pravde njegov sud.
»I ti poni odsud' dati grad i nas svih,
»(Pristani na taj blud) u ruke od sil tih;
»Stavmo se u volju njih, ali će skratiti
»Nagla smart tug ovih, al uza smaliti.«
205 Toj rekši, cviliti u carkvu stojući
I parste lomiti jaše jadajući,
K Bogu vapijući: »Bože, sagrišismo,
»Na zlo pristajući, nepravdu činismo!
»Krivinu tvorismo i s oci našimi
210 »Zakon ne spunismo; da ti, ki s' nad svimi,
»Milostiv ti primi na milost svih naju,
»Od ruk nas odnimi ki tebe ne znaju.
»Ki, prileć, ne daju da te čtuje tvoj stvor:
»Bog je sam, pravljaju, Nabukodonosor;
215 »Ne daj nas pod njih hor, jer će reć narod zal,
»Gdi je njihov nebotvor, ča jih ni pomogal?«
U veliku pečal, s plačnima očima
Ozija ustarhal staše meju njima,
Kako ki strašnima vitri zagonjen brod
220 Mev vali mnogima vodi prik slanih vod;
Svarta korablji hod ne kuda bi hotil,
Da dajuć jidrom god kud jih je duh zavil;
Li još se je usilil kokogod se oprit,
Dokla je tamun cil, ne hteć o školj udrit.
225 Simo-tamo pozrit ne staje jer vidi
Da mu se je borit s vitrom, s morem, s diždi;
Garbin hlopom hlidi a zvižju konopi,
Val rovući slidi, ter busa u popi.
Sve nebo poklopi oblak s tmasta lica,
230 Iz njega dižd kropi, mun'ja ga prosica;
Grom s triskom potica, strahotno tartnjući,
Preda, pada nica mornar li jidrući.

---

207. Bogu se mole grih svoj spovidajući.
217. Ozija bi pečalan čuvši da će se pridati; dali još imaše ufan'je u Bogu.

Than to be tormented, mouth agape, with nothing to drink;
Thus it is much the lesser labour to bear their chains,
Praising God in all things and His judgement of
    this matter.                                                     200
And thou now resolve to surrender the city and us all
(Acquiescing in this shame) into the hands of their troops.
Let us give ourselves up unto their will, that swift death
Might shorten these torments, or chains lessen them."

Having said this, they stood in their temple[18] and began   205
To wail and twist their fingers in lamentation,
And they cried to God:[19] "O God, we have sinned,
Insisting upon evil, we have transgressed Thy law!
We have committed an injustice and together with
    our forebears
Have not fulfilled Thy commandment; but Thou Who
    art above all,                                                 210
Mercifully accept us in Thy grace,
Deliver us from the hands of those who know Thee not.
Who breathing threats do not let Thy creation praise Thee:
Only, do they claim, is Nabuchodonosor god;
Place us not under their yoke, lest the wicked nation say,   215
Where then is their creator, why doth he not help them?"

In great grief, with tear-blinded eyes,[20]
Ozias stood terrified among them,
Like one who steereth a bark driven by fearsome winds
Midst mighty waves, across the briny deep;                   220
He changeth the ship's course not whither he wisheth,
But setteth free the ship's sails, as the spirit listeth:
Yet somehow he hath compelled himself to resist,
While the rudder is still whole, not wishing to dash
    against the reef,
Gazing constantly hither-thither, for he doth perceive       225
That he must contend with wind and sea and rain;
The sou'wester resoundeth noisily and the ropes whistle,
With a roar the wave beareth down and drummeth against
    the stern.
The whole sky is overcast with clouds of leaden aspect,
Rain poureth from it, lightnings rive it through;            230
With a crack thunder chaseth it, roaring fearfully,
The sailor still sailing yieldeth, prostrating himself.

---

18. (Marulić uses the word *crkva*, "church"–HC.)
19. They pray to God confessing their sin.
20. Ozias did lament hearing they would surrender; whether they still had faith in God.

　　　　　*Tako t' se obzirući, Ozija predaše*
　　　　　*Pogibil vidući, dali još uzdaše;*
235　　　*Zato govoraše, roneći suzami,*
　　　　　*Tere jih toljaše simi besidami:*
　　　　　*»Ne sobom, da vami, bratjo, pečalan bih,*
　　　　　　*»Zato vazda s nami Bog hoće biti, rih;*
　　　　　　*»I sada ja vas svih, ja životom mojim,*
240　　　　*»Iskupil bih od tih nevolj, i blagom svim.*
　　　　　*»To bit ne more, vim; da on ki stvori svit,*
　　　　　　*»To vazda reći smim, pomoć nam more bit;*
　　　　　　*»Zato nitkor zgubit ne htij čeljad i stan,*
　　　　　　*»I sam sebe ubit; počkajmo još pet dan,*
245　　　*»Jeda odrene van Bog saržbu tu od nas*
　　　　　　*»Ter svoj podstavi dlan uzdaržeć ov puk vas;*
　　　　　　*»Ako ne dojde spas ki mnju da će biti,*
　　　　　　*»Ča ste rekli danas, hoćemo stvoriti.«*
　　　　　*Hotiše starpiti svīt ovi Ozije*
250　　　*I jaše moliti da jim Bog barzije*
　　　　　*Pomoć svu podije i milo pohaja,*
　　　　　*Da jih ne ubije neprijatelj ni žaja. —*
　　　　　*Tada se nahaja Judit u gradu tom,*
　　　　　*Kâno svih nathaja lipostju, dobrotom,*
255　　　*Kâ živit životom odluči prečisto,*
　　　　　*Poče imit od kom udovičtva misto.*
　　　　　*Mnozi ju zaisto vlastele prosiše,*
　　　　　*Ona Bogu listo služiti želiše;*
　　　　　*Skrovišće imiše gori pod slimena,*
260　　　*Gdi Boga zoviše s rabom zatvorena.*
　　　　　*Hotin'ja putena usteza posteći,*
　　　　　*Strunami pletena vričišća noseći,*
　　　　　*Tege li težeći da nī telu pokoj,*
　　　　　*Almuštva čineći skupšćini uboškoj.*
265　　　*Živine velik broj muž bo nje ostavi*

---

237. **Prilika.** Odgovor Ozije grajanom ki se hotihu pridati.

244. Do pet staviše rok, ako jim dotla Bog ne pošalje pomoć, da se pridadu.

253. JUDITH.

Casting his eyes thus about, so too did Ozias surrender
Perceiving destruction, yet did he maintain hope;
Whereupon he spoke, shedding tears,                                235

And consoled them with these words:[21]
"Not for myself, brethren, but for you did I weep,
For, I have said, God will always be with us;
And now I would redeem you all with my life
From these miseries, and with all I own.                           240
I know this cannot be; but He Who made the world,
So I always dare to claim, may yet come to our aid;
Therefore let no man slay servants or household
Or even himself; let us endure yet five days,[22]
That God might turn this vexation from us,                         245
And, stretching out His palm, sustain all this people;
If the salvation doth not come that I believe will arrive,
What ye have said today, that will we do."

They agreed to follow Ozias' counsel
And began to pray that God more swiftly send                       250
His aid and mercifully visit them,
That neither the enemy nor thirst might slay them.

Now at that time in the city was Judith,[23]
Who exceeded all in beauty, goodness,
Who had decided to lead a life of chastity,                        255
From the time she had become a widow.
Many a powerful man had in truth sought her hand,
But she wished to serve only God.
She had a chamber upstairs, 'neath her roof,
Where, confined with her maidservant, she called on God.           260
She reined in the desires of the flesh with fasting,
Wearing sackcloth woven of horse-hair,
Or labouring, lest her body be at peace,
Distributing alms to the congregation of the poor.
For her husband had left her a great number of cattle              265

---

21. A comparison. Ozias' response to the inhabitants who wished to surrender.
22. They put the term at five, if God by then doth not send them help, they should surrender.
23. JUDITH.

  *I blago mnogo njoj kad se s njom rastavi;*
  *Da ona ne stavi u tom sarce svoje,*
  *Ner kô ljube pravi, vikomnje kôno je.*
 *Sva moć riči moje izreći ne umit*
270  *Pobožje koko je, cić koga gardi svit,*
  *Prem ako mladih lit biše i lipa stvora,*
  *Da od kriposti cvit — hći biše Merara,*
 *Ki zide od stara roda Simeona,*
  *Brata Isakara tere Zabulona;*
275  *Muža imi ona ki se zva Manases,*
  *Opslužeć zakona ki jim da Mojises.*
 *Ovogaj na poses, gdi se žetva tvori,*
  *Kad Sirij tere Pes najvećma uzgori,*
  *Moć toplin umori plamena vrućijih;*
280  *Martva ga zatvori grob njega starijih.*
 *Misec šesti lit trih jur biše napustil,*
  *Da biše on živih priminuvši pustil,*
  *Kada Judit sih dil potribu videći,*
  *Ča je Ozija ril, kara uzročeći,*
285  *Popom govoreći Kabru i Karmu dvim:*
  *»Kû rič izusteći Ozija reče svim,*
  *»Da grad dâ protivnim peti dan i petu noć,*
  *»Ako nam protiv njim ne pošlje Bog pomoć?*
 *»Tko ste, da ćete moć božju iskusiti,*
290  *»Ter svim vekšu nemoć, vekši gnjiv naditi?*
  *»Jer se rasarditi hoće tom ričju Bog,*
  *»Prî ner se smiliti, ni dati nam odlog.*
 *»Vele dvigoste rog, roke take upram*
  *»K Bogu, ki je svemog, da milost svû dâ nam,*
295  *»Ter da tad pride sam pomoć puku semu,*
  *»Kada je drago vam, ne kad je god njemu!*
 *»Milostan je u svemu, prošćen'je prosimo*
  *»Od togaj tere mu duše ponizimo;*

---

278. Sirij i Pas zovu se zvizde nike kê ističu kad su najveći krisi.

281. Jur bihu tri lita i šest miseci da biše obudovila Judita.

286. Judita kara jih cić roka toga od pet dan.

And numerous goods when he took leave of her;
But she placed not her heart thereupon,
But on that which the righteous love, what is eternal.
All the power of my words cannot proclaim
This piety of hers, for which she did scorn the world.        270
Though she was still young and of goodly countenance,
She was the very flower of firmness–the daughter of Merari,
Who was descended from the tribe of Simeon,
The brother of Issachar and Zebulon;
Her husband had been called Manasses,                          275
And he had observed the law given them by Moses.
Out in his fields, as the harvest was gathered,
When Sirius and the Dog Star were at the zenith,[24]
He was stricken by the power of the heat of their
   burning rays;
The grave of his ancestors closed over the dead man.          280
Three years and six months had already passed[25]
Since he had in departing left the realm of the living,
When Judith, perceiving the error of the people's deeds,
And what Ozias had said, meriting reproach,
Spoke to the priests, Chabris and Charmis:[26]                285

"What word is this that Ozias spoke to them,
That the city be delivered to the enemy on the fifth day
If God fail to send aid against them?
Who are ye, that ye would tempt the might of God,
And call down upon all greater helplessness, greater anger?   290
For God will sooner grow wrathful at these words
Than show us His mercy, or grant us reprieve.
Ye have been too bold in setting God a term,
Who is omnipotent, wherein He must show us mercy,
And that He come Himself to help His people                    295
When it suiteth you, not when it pleaseth Him!
He is merciful in all things, let us ask forgiveness
For this, and prostrate our souls before Him;

---

24. Sirius and the Dog Star are stars which appear at times of greatest crisis.
25. It was already three years and six months since Judith was widowed.
26. Judith reproacheth them for their term of five days.

»*S skrušen'jem molimo da po njega volju*
300 »*Lahkost oćutimo, odbivši nevolju;*
»*Da kako sad kolju oni nas ohoľ'jem.*
»*Tako padu u polju našim umiljen'jem;*
»*Jer izneviren'jem ne ockvarnismo se,*
»*Otac pristupljen'jem tuje boge prose,*
305 »*Koji grih podnose' oni tad u to dob*
»*Tarpiše angose, glad, meče i porob:*
»*Da nam je nepodob primat ner onoga,*
»*Abram, Isak, Jakob koga čtova Boga.*
»*Utišen'je toga čekajmo tarpljivo,*
310 »*Zla će nas ovoga zbavit milostivo,*
»*Tere će rugljivo zbiti pod moć nižu*
»*Svih, neprijaznivo ki se na nas dvižu.*
»*A sad božju hižu kino uzdaržite,*
»*K kim duše pribižu da jih očistite:*
315 »*Pristoji se, vite, popovstvu vašemu,*
»*Da sarca kripite vi puku našemu,*
»*Pomenak čine' mu od naših starijih;*
»*Jer Bog u ničemu zato nevolji jih,*
»*Da tim iskusi jih je li njih život prav,*
320 »*I je li vera u njih s ufan'jem ljubav.*
»*Abram u trudih stav i u skarbost mnogu,*
»*Kripak bi kako lav u služen'je Bogu;*
»*Pečali nalogu Isak, Jakob nosit*
»*Skazaše da mogu, a Bogu ne zgrišit.*
325 »*Mojses tokoj čini t', i svaki ushaja,*
»*Ki hti zlo pritarpit, da Bogu ugaja;*
»*A puk, ki ne haja, ner Boga da skusi,*
»*Saržba ga pohaja i samrt ga pokusi.*
»*Zato da ne strusi nami pomarmnjan'je,*
330 »*Činte, ner da skljusi nisko ponižan'je,*
»*Govore': karan'je božje to jest manje,*
»*Ner naše zgrišan'je i naše poganje.*
»*Bog nas bije hlanje nere dostojimo;*

---

305. Jer zavedeni biše u Babiloniju.
306. Angose: nevolje.
321. Popom govori: Abram, Isak, Jakob.

With repentance let us pray that according to His will
We might have relief and deliverance from our woes;  300
That just as they now pierce us in their arrogance,
So might they fall in battle through our humility;
For we have not polluted ourselves with disbelief,
Nor with the sin of fathers who worshipped alien gods,
Fathers bearing the consequences of their transgression
   aforetime,[27]  305
Who suffered miseries,[28] hunger, the sword and pillaging:
For it were unfitting for us to take any other
God but Him Whom Abraham, Isaac and
   Jacob worshipped.
Let us wait patiently for our consolation,
He will deliver us mercifully from this evil  310
And cast down in shame to the weaker force
All those who rise up against us in enmity.
And ye who care for the sanctuary of God,
To whom souls hasten that they might be cleansed:
It behooveth, see it clearly, your priestly office  315
To strengthen the hearts of this people,
By recalling the deeds of our forebears;
For God in their miseries did not indulge them,
But tested them for the righteousness of their lives,
Whether they had in themselves faith, hope and love.  320
Abraham in his trials and great grief,[29]
Was firm as a lion in the service of God;
The burden of sorrow Isaac and Jacob
Proved they could bear without sin before God.
Moses did the same, and each waxeth strong  325
Who is willing to bear evil in order to please God;
But the nation that seeketh nought but to tempt God,
Shall be visited by vexations and shall taste of death.
So that our murmuring therefore bring us not down,
Let us deeply bow in prayer,  330
Saying: God's punishment is less
Than our transgression and our lack of faith;
God chastiseth us more gently than we deserve,

---

27. For they had been led off to Babylon.
28. "Miseries": troubles. (Marulić explains the word "angose"–HC.)
29. She saith to the elders: Abraham, Isaac, Jacob.

>>Sarčno na nas zvanje da ga se bojimo,
335 »Da grih ostavimo, da bolji bivamo,
»A ne da zgubimo ča na svît imamo.« —
Pošadši k njoj tamo i Ozija sliša
Tuj rič, kâ ne samo da veće njim miša,
Ništar manje niša visoko hvalu nje,
340 Ka nišće ne zgriša ča biše istine se.
Zajedno s popi ste', riše: »Sve su prave,
»Judita, riči te kê s' rekla sad; zdrave
»Da budu daržave i mi, moli za nas:
»Svetosti tve slave znane su po svît vas.«
345 Ona reče: »Danas ča sam rekla godi,
»Kako zna svaki nas od Boga da shodi,
»Tako po sej škodi hoćete vidit stvar,
»Kû misal ma svodi, da ni ner božji dar.
»Sada imijte var višnjega moliti,
350 »Da ruku mû prostar, rači to stvoriti;
»Ostavte hotiti znati misal moju,
»Na vratoh siditi hoćete noć ovu;
»A kada ja pojdu vanka s Abrom mojom,
»Dokla opet dojdu, svi vi s družbom svojom
355 »Molte svetom molbom za nas oca Boga
»S umiljenom pojom i s skrušen'ja moga.« —
»Poj i Bog zla toga po te oslobodi
»Jur puka ovoga!« Ozija tako di:
»Zbogom poj i hodi i kuda godir greš,
360 »Vazdi te pohodi, vazdi slavom ureš'.
»I pri nere umreš, on čin', da dila, kô
»Godir stvorit napreš, glas dvignut visoko
»I prostart široko po svitu bude znan.«
Govoriv to toko, s popovi pojde van,
365 Misleći duboko, ostaviv nju na stan.

---

341. Ozija s popi pohvališe karan'je Juditino.
350. Judita dâ jim red da za nju mole i su noć propuste vanka grada.
364. Blagosloviv ju, od nje se diliše.

Maketh us sincerely mindful that we fear Him,
That we leave off sinning, that we mend our ways,               335
And that we lose not what we have in this world."

Ozias too, having gone to her, heard these words,
Which, though they upset him all the more,
Nevertheless he did praise to the heights,
Praised her who spake nothing but the truth.                    340
Those who stood with the priests said:[30] "All thy words,
Judith, which thou now speakest are true;
That all lands thrive and we, too, pray thus for us:
The holiness of thy glory is known throughout the world."
She saith: "Whatever I have spoken this day                     345
As each of us knoweth, it cometh from God,
So that after this trial ye shall see that the thing
Which my mind hath fashioned is nought but God's gift.
Now take care to pray to the Almighty
That, stretching forth His hand, He deign do this;[31]          350
Leave off wishing to know any further my mind,
Sit ye at the gate all night long.
And when I go outside with my servant Abra,
Till I come back again, ye with the whole company
Of the people pray prayerfully to God for us                    355
With hymns of humility and great repentance."

"Go, and through thee may God swiftly free
His people of this evil!" saith Ozias:
"Go with God and whithersoever thou goest,
May He go with thee, and adorn thee with glory.                 360
And before thou diest, may He deign that the tale
Of the work that thou essayest to do be shouted out,
Bruited about, and known throughout the world."
Having spoken thus, he went out with the priests,
Sunk deeply in thought, leaving her in her room.[32]

---

30. Ozias and the elders praise Judith's reproach.
31. Judith commandeth them to pray for her and to let her that night out of the city.
32. Having blessed her, they depart from her.

## LIBRO ČETVARTO

      Oni odašadši, Judit u komori
      Svojoj tad pošadši, dviže ruke gori
      Ter tako govori lugom potrusivši
      Svû glavu odzgori, kip vrićom odivši:
5    »Bože, ki stvorivši svaka, obladaš svim,
      »I sve naredivši, zakon si dal tvojim,
      »Dal si ocem mojim meč kim odvratiše
      »Rugo i silu onim ki silu činiše;
      »Ki ovašćiniše sestru njih, u zlo jih
10   »Tišće, i vidiše žen i hćeri svojih
      »Od sebe rastojih, blago razdiljeno
      »U ruke slug tvojih, tobom dopušćeno:
      »Tebe umiljeno, Gospodine, molju,
      »Pogledaj smiljeno na našu nevolju;
15   »Otpusti zlu volju i rabi Juditi
      »Pomozi, kâ volju tvu želim spuniti
      »Rači se smiliti, milostiv bo jesi,
      »Sve mož' učiniti, zla od nas odnesi;
      »Desnom tvojom stresi asirske sile sad,
20   »U zgibil zanesi, kako egipske tad
      »Tirahu puk tvoj kad s oružjem tekući

---

    5. Molitva Juditina.
    9. Ki ovašćiniše: budući Jakob s narodom svojim kon grada Salem u zemlju kananejsku, Sikem, sin Emora poglavice od grada, zagledav Dinu, hćer njegovu, ugrabi ju i pomča u grad. Za tim ju isprosi u Jakoba da mu bude žena, i prijaše obrizovan'je. Ništar manje tretji dan Simeon i Levi, bratja nje, s ljudmi svojimi s oružjem skočiše u grad i porubiše, muže pobiše, žene i dicu odvedoše. Dinu oteše i pojdoše.
    20. Kad Čarljeno more potopi egipsku vojsku kâ tiraše puk božji.

## Book The Fourth

Once they had gone, Judith returned to her chamber,
Raised her hands on high
And spoke thus, sprinkling her forehead
With ash and arraying her body with sackcloth:[1]

"O God Who didst make all, dost rule all,     5
And Who, having finished all, gavest the law to Thy people,
Gavest the sword to my forefathers, by which they
    did turn away
The reproach and violence of them who committed
    violence;
Them who defiled my forebears' sister,[2] Thou didst
    press upon,
And they saw their wives and daughters     10
Torn from them, their wealth divided
Into the hands of Thy servants, as Thou didst allow:
Thee, O Lord, do I humbly beseech,
Behold with mercy our sorry state;
Forget Thy wrath and to Thy servant Judith     15
Who desireth to do Thy will, render aid.
Deign to have mercy upon us, for Thou art gracious,

Thou art all-powerful, cast this evil from us;
Shatter now with Thy right hand the Assyrian forces,
Lead them to destruction, as once the Egyptians,[3]     20
Who did pursue and press Thy people with arms,

---

1. Judith's prayer.
2. "Them who defiled": Jacob was with his people near the city of Salem in the land of Caanan, when Shechem, the son of Hamor, the prince of the country, saw Dinah, Jacob's daughter, seized her and fled to the city. Afterwards he did ask Jacob for her to be his wife, and he was circumcised. Nevertheless, on the third day, Simeon and Levi, her brothers, together with their men and arms, came boldly upon the city and spoiled it, slew the men, carried off the women and children. They rescued Dinah and went out.
3. When the Red Sea drowned the Egyptian troops who were pursuing the people of God.

»*I svaki, karvi rad, naglo napirući,*
»*Ter se uzdajući u kola, u konje,*
»*U silu, li mnjući, tud'je potarti nje;*
25 »*Da sa strane gornje pozrivši tva milost,*
»*U prezdan'je donje pade njih oholost;*
»*Pomanjka jim jakost, nitkor se ne varnu,*
»*Ne osta jih ni kost, svih voda pogarnu:*
»*Tako da posarnu ovi, moj Bože čin,*
30 »*Ki misle da zgarnu sada nas s ovih stin;*
»*Ti jur njimi privin, kolik je, da znaju,*
»*U njih uzdan'ju hin ki u se uzdaju;*
»*Ki se uznišaju kopji ter strilami,*
»*Šćiti, kih višaju o vratu prik rami,*
35 »*I britci sabljami i konji barzimi,*
»*Mnogimi silami i ljudmi hrabrimi,*
»*Ne znajuć nad svimi da si Gospodin ti,*
»*Da s' pomoć pravimi, ne tome ki prav ni:*
»*Poni ki vo svih ji, nigdare karvi sit,*
40 »*Ti silu njega htij silom tvojom slomit;*
»*Ki tempal razorit jest se zahvalio,*
»*Sveta tvâ ockvarnit kâ s' ti posvetio;*
»*Krov, ki je sad cio, stukši ga razvrići,*
»*Mečem svojih sio oltar tvoj prisići:*
45 »*Ti učin odsići njegove gardosti*
»*Mečem kim posići priti tve svetosti;*
»*Pridaj mu sliposti, neka ga zadiju*
»*Mrižom me liposti i zamkom očiju.*
»*Kad s njima uzbesiju, da riči jazika*
50 »*Moga se zabiju u sarce človika,*
»*I ljubav velika smami ga tudije,*
»*Tako da do vika ne znat bude gdi je.*
»*Čini u mni smin'je, sarce da s' utvardi*
»*I stanovitije da njega pogardi;*
55 »*A da ga rastvardi skoro desna ovaj*
»*I sasvim ogardi, kripost joj ti podaj.*
»*Takova stvar i taj po tebi stvorena*
»*Biti će po vas kraj slava tvoga imena.*

---

43. Krov: tempal.

Each one of them bloodthirsty, racing headlong,
And trusting in chariot and horse,
Believing in his own strength, he sought to slay them
   there;
But Thy mercy looked down from on high,                    25
And their arrogance was thrust into the bottomless pit;
Their strength failed, not one of them returned,
Nor did one bone remain, the waters swallowed them all;
Likewise, my God, make these stumble,
Who think to dislodge us now from these cliffs;            30
Smite them then that they might know
The vanity of their trust who trust in themselves;
Who boast themselves of their spears and arrows,
Of the shields that they bear o'er neck and shoulder,
Of their sharp swords and swift horses,                    35
Of their great multitudes and brave men,
But do not know that over all Thou art Lord,
That Thou art help to the righteous, not to the wicked:
Cast down therefore with Thy strength the strength
Of him who consumeth all, nor hath his fill of blood;      40
Who hath sworn to destroy Thy sanctuary,
And defile the holy things Thou hast consecrated;
To overturn and destroy Thy tabernacle's[4] integrity,
To cut off with the sword of his force Thine altar:
Now cut Thou off with the sword of his pride               45
Him who hath come to pollute Thy holy places;
Increase his blindness, let him be ensnared
By the net of my beauty, by the wiles of mine eyes.
When I converse with him, may the words of my mouth
Pierce the heart of that man;                              50
And may a great love seduce him then
So that he may no longer know where he stand.
Confirm boldness in me, so my heart might be strong
And might despise him the more surely;
And that my right hand may quickly soften him              55
And deprive him of his comeliness, give it Thy strength.
Such a thing, when it hath been done by Thee,
Will throughout the land be the glory of Thy name,

---

4. "Tabernacle": the temple.

»Ako jedna žena ubije muža, kim
60  »Sad je pristrašena Zemlja s narodom svim.
»Ni jakost tvoja, vim, u mnoštvo nišćih ljud',
»Ni oružja ni s tim u barzih konji trud,
»Da u volje tvoje sud, kim si vazda nizil
»Svaku oholu ćud, umiljenu višil.
65  »Vazda s' milostiv bil i tisih molitav
»Vazda si uslišil: ti sada uslišav
»Rabu tvoju, postav rič u ustih mojih,
»U sarcu razum prav, moć u rukah ovih:
»Hiža svetinj tvojih vavik sveta da je
70  »I u narodih svih da te svak poznaje,
»Svak te spovidaje, reče: Ovo je Bog,
»Koga vlast svuda je i ki je sam svemog.«
Takoj se ona pomog svetimi molbami,
Prostarv kolina nog, dviže gori rami,
75  I sašad skalami, Abru svoju dozva,
Kâ, jer pod svitami spaše, jedva se ozva
Ona ju ne psova, da reče: »Opravi se
»I pojti van krova sa mnom sad spravi se.«
Toj rekši, izvi se iz vriće i vodom
80  Po puti umi se i namaza vonjom.
Splete glavu kosom, vitice postavi,
Kontuš s urehom svóm vazam na se stavi;
S ošvom ruke spravi, uši s userezmi,
Na nogah napravi čizmice s podvezmi.
85  S urehami tezmi, ča mi je viditi,
Dostojna bi s knezmi na sagu siditi;
I jošće hoditi na pir s kraljicami
I čtovana biti meju banicami.
Zlatimi žicami sjahu se poplitci,
90  A trepetljicami zvonjahu uvitci;
Stahu zlati cvitci po svioni sviti,
Razlici, ne ritci po skutih pirliti,
Svitlo čarljeniti jâ rubin na parstih,
Cafir se modriti, bilit na rukavih

---

78. Van krova: van kuće.
81. Kako se ureši Judita.

If a woman kill the man who bringeth terror
To this land and its inhabitants.　　　　　　　　　　　　　60
For I know that Thy power standeth not in multitudes,
Nor in arms nor the strength of swift horses,
But in the justice of Thy will, by which alway
Thou casteth down each proud character, lifteth up
　　the oppressed.
Thou hast ever been merciful and the prayers of the
　　meek　　　　　　　　　　　　　　　　　　　　　65
Thou hast ever heeded: heed now Thy servant,
Put Thy word on her lips,
A right mind in her heart, strength in these hands:
May the house of Thy sanctuary ever be holy,
That among the gentiles each acknowledge Thee,　　　70
Each confess Thee, saying: This is God,
Whose power is everywhere, Who alone is omnipotent."

Empowering herself thus with prayer,
She stretched out her legs, cast back her shoulders,
And descended the stairs, calling her Abra,　　　　　　75
Who, wrapped in her blankets, barely heard the summons.
She did not chastise her, but said: "Make thyself ready,
And prepare to go with me out-of-doors."[5]
That said, she undid the sackcloth and washed
Her body all over with water, and anointed herself
　　with oil.　　　　　　　　　　　　　　　　　　80
She braided the hair of her head, and donned garlands,[6]
And selecting garments of gladness, she adorned herself,
Putting cloth of gold on her arms, rings on her ears,
Fastened light shoes upon her feet.
With such adornments, so seemeth it to me,　　　　　85
She was worthy to sit with princes 'fore the hearth,
Or to attend feasts with queens,
And to be in repute among the wives of governors.
Her tresses shone with thread of gold,
And her locks did resound with bangles:　　　　　　90
Golden florets flowered on her silken skirt,
Many and varied were the colours woven in her dress.
The ruby on her fingers waxed a bright red,
The sapphire darkened blue; on her sleeves

---

5. "Out-of-doors": outside the house.
6. How Judith adorned herself.

95     Biser i na buštih, i sve od zlatih plas
        Sjati se na bedrih prehitro kovan pas.
    Velik urehe glas, da liposti veći,
        Kâ biše kako klas iz trave resteći,
    Al kami, ki steći u zlato, zlatu dâ,
100     Izvarsno svitleći, da zlato većma sja:
    Tako t' ona prida uresi krasosti
        Poveće ner prija od njeje liposti.
    I to ne bi dosti, kako pismo pravi,
        Bog njeje svitlosti uljudstva pristavi;
105     Jer te take spravi ne bihu od bludi,
        Da svete ljubavi i pravednih ćudi:
    Zato joj posudi da tko ju ugleda,
        Svak joj se počudi i za njom pogleda.
    Poni kad se zgleda spravna jur kako pir,
110     Pripravi obeda: kruh, uli, pargu, sir,
    I vinca malo mir u miščić, pak zamak
        U dvanjkah vas taj žir, Abri bi naramak.
    Toj ti na ramo ustak, Abra prida stupi
        I Judit nju potak, za njom ti postupi.
115     Kada jur nastupi na gradne zaklopi,
        Zastaše u skupi Oziju sa popi;
    Vratar vrat otklopi, svi se ustupiše:
        One steruć stopi, naprid postupiše;
    Tad se uščudiše svi, vidiv Juditu,
120     Toko lipa biše i u takovu svîtu.
    Liplja, mnju, na svitu nî bila kû kralj svet
        Vidiv u pohitu dvimi grisi bi spet;
    Al ona, kûno uzêt ljubavju vzê Sikem,
        S česa rasut i klet osta s njim grad Salem.

---

101. Kako Judita veće liposti da uresi ner ureha njoj, budi da vele biše urešena.

102. Prilika.

121. Ovo biše Bersaba, žena Urije, kû David vidivši obljubi, a dâ red da on zgine u vojsci. Dvima grisi bi spet: živodiostvom i ubojstvom.

123. Sikem: ov ugrabi Dinu, od kê smo rekli zgara na naglavu ovoga libra.

And breast flashed the white pearl, and wrought of gold 95
Links, the cleverly fashioned cincture did shine on
   her hips.
Great was her adornment, greater yet the beauty
Of her who was like a ripened ear 'midst the grasses,
Or a precious stone, set in gold, which alloweth
In the brilliance of its light, the gold to shine the more: 100
Thus did she lend more loveliness to her attire[7]
Than did her attire add to her own beauty.[8]
Nor was that the end, as Scripture doth tell,
God added to her brilliance still more charm;
For such allures were not deceitful, 105
But filled with sacred love and righteous notions:
So that He ordained that all who saw her
Be amazed at her and stare after her.
When then she had prepared herself, she did lay
Out a meal like a feast: bread, oil, parched corn, cheese, 110
And a small measure of wine she did pack,
And put them in a bag and laid them upon Abra.
She placed them on her shoulder, Abra set out first,
Judith, urging her on, followed behind.
And when they did reach the gates of the city, 115
They encountered Ozias together with the ancients;
The guard drew the gate, all let her pass:
The two women, stepping out, moved on ahead;
Then they were all amazed who saw Judith,
So beauteous was she, and in such attire. 120
More beauteous, I believe, than she whom that holy king[9]
Did once see, and he was snared in double sin;
Or than she whom Shechem, smitten with love, did take[10]
And was destroyed and cursed, along with his town
   of Salem.

---

7. How Judith lent more beauty to her attire than it to her, though she was well attired.
8. A comparison.
9. This was Bath-sheba, Uriah's wife, whom David, when he saw her, did love, and commanded that Uriah perish in battle. He was bound by two sins: adultery and murder.
10. Shechem: he seized Dinah, about whom we spoke above at the beginning of this book.

125    Al kû vidiv ognjem jur studena starost
        Užga se dviju prem, kim sva laž da žalost;
        Ali kûno hitrost Amona prihini,
        Ki meča ne bi prost dilj sile kû čini.
        Al kê toko scini Asuer uljudstvo,
130    Da na njoj zamini kraljice oholstvo;
        Al cić kê obilstvo od filistinskih njiv
        Požga, pustiv mnoštvo lisic, Sansonov gnjiv.
        Al ona, koj odkriv, otajstva istinu
        I u krilo se uviv, izgubi jačinu. —
135    Da ovih krivinu, u kih jest, odkladam;
        Lipost, ne rič inu, Juditi prikladam.
        Kôj jošće nakladam, ako nî laž i hin,
        Kupeći ča skladam od poetskih tašćin:
        Mnju ti bi Apolo lin tirati Dafnu bil,
140    Tad kon tesalskih stin ovu da bi vidil.
        Siringu bi otpustil sin Merkurijev Pan,
        Ugledal da bi bil ovu gredući van;

---

125. Ovo je Susana, žena Joakina, na kû se starci namuraše; i ona ne pristavši k njim, nalagaše na nju, i našad u laž, pobijeni biše kamen'jem. Zato di kîm sva laž da žalost.

127. Ovo je bila Tamar, hći Davidova od Maake, na kû se namura Amon, sin Davidov od Akinoe. Učini se nemoćan i dâ red da mu ona nastoji. I učini joj silu. Zato brat nje Absalon, jer bihu jedne matere, zvavši ga na večeru, čini ga ubiti.

129. Asuer, kralj od Persije, kraljicu Vastu pusti jer se ne haja priti kad ju zoviše. Na misto nje oda svih obra Hesteru Židovinku, jer najliplja biše.

132. Ovu obljubi Sanson; i on odašadši, poja ona drugoga muža. Kad se varnu, ne daše mu k njoj; zato on lisicam na rep oganj navezavši, pusti u žita njih i požga.

134. Ovo je bila Dalida, kojoj Sanson pravivši u čem biše jačina njegova, uspi ga na krilo, ostriže mu vlase, osta nejak i uhitiše ga neprijatelji.

140. Poete govore da Apolo zagledav Dafnu, hćer Peneja, jer u svoj Tesaliji biše najlipša, jâ tirati. Ona pobiže i obrati se u javor.

141. Tako je Pan tira Siringu cića liposti; i ona, da ju ne uhiti, obrati se u tarst.

Or she whom the two did see, and their cold old years[11]  125
Were enflamed, and their own lie brought grief;
Or she whom the craftiness of Amnon did seduce,[12]
But he was not spared the sword for the violence that
   he did.
Or she whose allures Ahasuerus valued so[13]
That he descried in her the boldness of a queen;  130
Or she for whom the rich harvest of Philistine fields
Samson's anger did consume as he released the foxes.[14]
Or she who discovering the truth of his secret
Ensnared him in her lap and robbed him of his strength.[15]
But the sinful ways of these, as they were, I put aside,  135
Beauty, and nothing more, to Judith I ascribe.
To her I also add, if it be not lie or delusion,
What I collect and compose from the vanities of poets:
I believe Apollo would not have chased Daphne
Had he first seen Judith at the crags of Thessaly.[16]  140
Mercury's son Pan would have let Syrinx go,[17]
Had he espied Judith coming forth to him;

---

11. This is Susanna, Joachim's wife, for whom the elders were enflamed; but she did not submit to them, and they slandered her, and their lie being found out, they were stoned to death. Therefore saith he: "and their own lie brought grief."
12. This was Tamar, the daughter of David and Ma'acah, for whom Amnon became enflamed, David's son by Achinoe. He pretended to be ill and commanded her to wait on him. And he raped her. Therefore her brother Absalom, for they were of one mother, summoned him to supper and had him killed.
13. Ahasuerus, the King of Persia, dismissed Queen Vashti for she would not come when he summoned her. In her place he chose from among all the women Esther the Jewess, who was the most beautiful.
14. Samson did love her; and when he left, she took another husband. When he returned, they would not let him in to her; therefore he tied fire to the tails of foxes, and let them into their crops and burned them.
15. This was Delilah, in whose lap, after that he had confided to her wherein lay his strength, he did fall asleep, and she shoar his hair, he became weak and his enemies overpowered him.
16. The poets say that Apollo, having seen Daphne, the daughter of Peneus, who was the most beautiful girl in all Thessaly, began to pursue her. She fled and was changed into a laurel.
17. Thus did Pan pursue Syrinx for her beauty; she too, so that she might not be captured, was turned into a reed.

Po Cinte gore stran kadano lovljaše
Diana luk napan, taka se vijaše.
145 Kada se boraše za s Dijanirom stat
Herkules, kôj mnjaše da par neće postat:
Kip, obraz tere vrat ove zgledal da bi,
Vargal bi se navrat, al se boril ne bi.
Ča veće dim tebi? Paris taku ženu
150 Imil da bi sebi, pustil bi Helenu,
Kû Garci odvedenu, jer opet nimaše,
Troju podsedenu deset lit arvaše.
Ako poni staše zamamljeni, ove
Kad lice zgledaše, s Ozijom popove,
155 Ne čudo, jer, slove koga moć, Bog tadi
Nje gizde takove lipostju obnadi.
Nitkor ju ne zadi ni riču ni stvarju,
I stupiv nazadi, da projde, pušćav ju
Rekoše: »Možav ju, Bože otac naših,
160 »Oda zla izbav ju i od tih sil strašnih;
»Misal nje kriposnih dili ti napuni
»I milost daj da njih svaršeno ispuni;
»Da glas nje pripuni i zemlju i kamen,
»Sama se ukruni sa svetimi. Amen.«
165 Jur sunčeni plamen, vodeći s sobom dan,
Od zvizd jasnih zlamen takjaše, grede 'van:
Bižeć na nižnji stan noć s čarnimi koli,
Nošaše donjim san, ako su ki doli.
Kad ljudi oholi ki stražu bljudoše,

---

144. Ovo je Diana, božica prelipa, kâ s divicami love lovljaše.

145. Dijaniru, hćer Eneja, jer vele lipa biše, mnozi prošahu. Otac odluči dati ju tomu ki dobude boreći se. Bori se Herkules sa Akelojom i dobi ga. Da bi di ovu vidil, ali se ne bi boril, ali bi se vargal da ostavi nju, a pojde za ovom.

150. Paris, sin kralja Prijama, odvede Helenu u Troju; ne hti ju vratiti. Ćić toga Garci podsedoše Troju. Deset lit ju arvaše, napokon prijaše i rasuše.

159. Blagosloviše Juditu kad izide iz grada.

165. Sunce istekši, straža srite Juditu.

Like Diana, hunting on the slopes of Cynthus,[18]
And stretching her bow, did she carry herself forth.
When Hercules fought to approach Deanira,[19]  145
He believed none would be born to equal her in beauty:
Were he though to catch sight of this figure, face and neck,
He would stop, nor would he battle on.
What more can I tell thee? Had Paris such a wife,
He would have left Helen,[20]  150
For whom the Greeks, from whom she had been abducted,
Having her no more, besieged Troy ten years long.
If then the ancients stood in awe with Ozias
When they caught sight of her,
It is not surprising, for God, Whose power is well-known,  155
Did embellish her adornments with beauteousness.
None made to touch her with word or gest,
And standing aside to let her pass,
They said:[21] "Give her strength, Lord God of our fathers,
Preserve her from evil and all fearful forces;  160
Fill her mind with thoughts of mighty deeds
And give her the grace to perform them effectually;
So that her renown fill earth and firmament,
And that she receive the crown of the saints. Amen."

Already the sun's ray, bringing on the day,[22]  165
Matched the brightness of the lust'rous stars as they left:
Racing to her subterranean abode, night on her black chariot
Was carrying sleep to those below, if there are ought.
When the arrogant men who kept the Assyrian guard,

---

18. This is Diana, a most lovely goddess, who did hunt with her maidens.
19. Deanira, Aeneas' daughter, in that she was very beautiful, was sought by many. Her father resolved to give her to him who won her in battle. Hercules fought with Achilleus and conquered him. This meaneth: had he seen Judith, either he would not have fought, or he would have resolved to leave Deanira and follow Judith.
20. Paris, King Priam's son, carried off Helen to Troy; he did not want to return her. Therefore did the Greeks besiege Troy. Ten years did they do battle before they took and destroyed it.
21. . They blessed Judith as she went out of the city.
22. As the sun riseth, the guards encounter Judith.

170         *Ophode okoli Juditu sritoše,*
            *Slišat ju zajdoše: »Od kud greš i kamo?*
           *»Ća t' jime,« rekoše, »pravi nam, da znamo.«*
        *Ona reče: »Ovamo od Betulije sam*
           *»I put je moj tamo k vašim poglavicam;*
175         *Ostaviv grad i hram, s životom bižim tja,*
           *»Jer će se dati vam; Judit se zovu ja.*
        *»A da sa mnom sada ova drúga verna*
           *»Ne ostane zada sasvima čemerna;*
           *»Doprit Oloferna ne brante mi, molim,*
180         *»Vlast njega nesmerna da pozna ča kolim.*
        *»Reći će: toj volim; jer mu ću skazati*
           *»Ća će bit oholim, i kako će jati*
           *»Ov grad, a nimati škodu ni trud velik,*
           *»Tako da s te rati ne zgine ni človik.« —*
185         *Ne bî ti ner tolik tada govor njeje;*
           *Oni hip nikolik postaše glede' je,*
           *Čude' se od kude je stvoren'je, od kega*
           *Sve od svita meje nimaju lipljega;*
        *Pak rekoše: »S tvega premudra i smina*
190         *»Činjen'ja od svega biti će t' načina,*
           *»Kû želiš, ne ina; toj on čas oćutiš,*
           *»Ki prid gospodina našega postupiš.*
        *»Dobro ne izustiš da će ti sve dati,*
           *»Ća godir obljubiš i budeš pitati;*
195         *»Jer će dostojati tî razum, tâ lipost,*
           *»Da bude imati svaku čast i milost.«*
        *Govore' toj, linost s njom pojti nimiše,*
           *Gledaje' nje svitlost svi se zamamiše;*
           *Kud se obratiše, hode' meju vojskom,*
200         *Svim oči zaniše, svaki zarča za njom.*
        *Greduć uprav stazom, dojdoše k šatoru,*
           *I on ju prid sobom zazva u komoru,*
           *Ki polje i goru mnoštvom svojih sio,*
           *Kako ti govoru, biše pokrilio.*
205         *Kad ju je vidio, s parvoga pozora*

---

173. Kako se Judita zgovara sa stražami.
202. Oloferne ju čini priti prid sobom.

Encountered Judith and surrounded her, 170
They began to ask: "Whence comest, whither goest thou?
What might be thy name," quoth they, "tell us that we
    might know."
She said:²³ "I come hither from Bethulia,
And my path taketh me to your chiefs;
Having left town and hearth, I run for my life hither, 175
For they shall be delivered unto you; Judith is my name.
And so that this my faithful friend
Remain not behind in consternation,
Do not forbid me, I pray you, to go to Holofernes,
So that his immeasurable power might learn what
    I desire. 180
He shall say: I relish this; for I will tell him
How he might boast himself and how he might take
The city, nor shall he suffer harm or pain,
So that in the battle not one man of his be lost."
Her speech then was not more than that; 185
They stood a few moments gazing at her,
And marveling at this creature, than whom
All the bounds of the world have none more beauteous;
And they said: "For thy wise and bold
Action it shall be done completely 190
As thou desirest, not otherwise; this thou shalt perceive
The moment thou comest before our master.
Before thou even speakest, he will give thee all
Thou mightest desire or ask for;
For thy wisdom and beauty shall suffice 195
That he might attain every honour and grace."
Having said that, they set out with her nor did delay,
All were beside themselves as they gazed on her beauty;
Where e'er they went, walking among the troops,
All turned their eyes toward her, did follow after her. 200
They took the straight path, and came to his tent,
And he called her into his presence in his chamber,²⁴
He, as I have said, covered field and mountain
With the multitude of his armies.
When he did see her, from the very first sight, 205

---

23. How Judith addresseth the guards.
24. Holofernes hath her brought before him.

        *Ranu je oćutio ljubvena umora;*
        *Staše kako gora, sobom ne krećući,*
        *Oči ne zatvora, k njoj jih upirući:*
        *Tako sta tarnući serifski gospodin,*
210    *Medusu kažući njemu Danaje sin.*
        *Pod šator u osin ki stahu knezove,*
        *Svi se okolo sklin, gledaše obraz ove*
        *I riše: »Takove ako se tuj goje,*
        *»Podstupmo gradove i ki u njih stoje:*
215    *»Arvanje i boje ni triba odnimit,*
        *»Grade, horu toje dokol budemo imit.*
        *»A tko se neće bit i vazda u svaki boj,*
        *»Dobrovoljno hodit zacić tacih gospoj?«*
        *Ona ti meju toj prid Oloferna stav,*
220    *Sideća na pristoj, pisan vàs kako pav;*
        *Jer ga tkalac otkav, komu ne biše par*
        *U asirsku daržav, biše jimio mar*
        *Naštrikat cvitja bar svilami razlici*
        *I zlatom i još zgar dragimi kamici.*
225    *Tuj poni u lici pozriv ga Judita,*
        *Pade k zemlji nici vele uhilita:*
        *Poklon hitra svita biše, kim ga dvori;*
        *On se rukom hita i reče: »Stan gori!«*
        *Paka joj govori: »Budi dobrovoljna,*
230    *»Bit ćeš u mom dvori prijata i voljna;*
        *»Ni ina nevoljna zemlja u istinu,*
        *»Ner služit zlovoljna momu gospodinu:*
        *»I puk tvoj gardinu da ne skaže k meni,*
        *»Ne bi mû jačinu kušali tužbeni;*
235    *»Bili bi blaženi u svem svomu horu,*
        *»Budući službeni Nabuk'donosoru.*
        *»A sada da t' stvoru milost kû t' obitam,*

---

210. Prilika. Ovo je bio Polidektes, kralj od Serifa otoka, ki se okameni kad mu ukaza glavu od Meduze Perzej, sin Jovetov i Danaje; kû glavu tko godi vijaše, zakamenjaše se. To pišu poete. Zato dî ovdi, da Oloferne sta kako zakameniv se gledajući Juditu.
226. Kako se Judita pokloni Olofernu.
229. Oloferne govori Juditi.

He felt the wound of love's deadly sting;
He stood firm as a mountain, nor did he move,
He blinked not, but fixed his gaze upon her:
Thus was the lord of Seriphus struck dumb
When Danae's son showed him the head of Medusa.[25]   210
'Neath the tent, where in the shadows stood his princes,
In a flock, they stared into her face
And said: "If such women are raised here,
Let us besiege their towns and those who abide in them:
Nor should we neglect fighting and battling   215
Till we conquer their cities and all of their land.
For who will not fight, nor of his own free will
Go to battle at any time for the sake of such women?"
She in the meanwhile stood before Holofernes
Seated on his throne, brilliant as a peacock;   220
For a weaver who had no equal
In all of Assyria had bedecked him, taken great care
To adorn him with an abundance of flowers in
   coloured silk
And gold, topped off with precious stones.
Here then Judith looked him in the face,   225
Fell prostrate on the earth in great humility:[26]
'Twas the bow of crafty folk, who did seek to suade him;
He stretched out his hand and said: "Arise!"
Then he said to her:[27] "Be of good comfort,
In my court thou shalt be safeguarded and free;   230
In truth no other land is unfree
Except the one that be unwilling to serve my lord;
And had thy people not set light by me,
They would not, lamenting, have tasted of my strength;
They would have been joyful throughout all their land,   235
Being the servants of great Nabuchodonosor.
And now that I might do thee the kindness
   that I promised,

---

25. A comparison. This was Polydectes, the King of the Isle of Seriphus, who did turn to stone when Perseus, the son of Zeus and Danae, showed him the head of Medusa; whose head whoever looketh upon it turneth to stone. Thus the poets write. It meaneth here that Holofernes stood as if turned to stone when he looked upon Judith.
26. How Judith did reverence Holofernes.
27. Holofernes addresseth Judith.

»*I kako t' govoru, da t' se ne izvitam,*
»*Rec mi ča te pitam: za ki uzrok onuj*
240 »*Stran, za kù pohitam, ostaviv dojde tuj?«*
Ona malo otuj stupiv, dviže oči
  Tere tiho uz tuj rič riči potoči:
  »*Ako smi uz oči gospodina svoga*
  »*Raba da mu soči, sliši svîta moga;*
245 »*Jer gospodstva tvoga velikost ako će*
  »*Dostojat se toga, ča želi, znat hoće.*
  »*Sa tvoje pomoće kralj Nabuk'donosor*
  »*Ne samo ovo će, da svita steć prostor,*
  »*I ne listo taj dvor hoće mu služiti*
250 »*Po tebi, da vas stvor i zimi i liti;*
  »*Jer je po svem sviti glas tvoje hrabrosti,*
  »*Smin'ja, sile, svisti i svake mudrosti.*
  »*Da neka t' ludosti skažem puka moga,*
  »*Ki tvojoj milosti ne da mista svoga:*
255 »*Rasardil je Boga ki po prorocih svih*
  »*Priti da će s toga pridati tebi njih.*
  »*A jer znaju svoj grih, zato t' trepe strahom,*
  »*U plač obrativ smih, muče se uzdahom;*
  »*Telo sarši mahom, obraz je gladan, žut,*
260 »*Jazik popal prahom, žadan, ližući mut.*
Jure od skota mut ožimlju, ophode
  »*Kupeći ga u skut, jer pripuše vode;*
  »*Stada i stad plode klat su odlučili,*
  »*Karv njih, kâ je gode, hlepeć da bi pili,*
265 »*Hlepeć da bi jili, riše da straćeni*
  »*Budu ki su bili sudi posvećeni,*
  »*Zlati ter zlaćeni, za vino i žito,*
  »*A bit će ockvarnjeni da jih taknu listo.*
»*Ne bud sumnjen ništo, s toga će smagnuti,*
270 »*Kako s' na to misto, svi će poginuti;*
  »*Zato odbignuti odlučih i k tebi*
  »*Totuj pribignuti da me primeš k sebi.*
»*Ni to bilo ne bi, ako bi naš on Bog,*
  »*Kino je na nebi, ne dvigal na njih rog;*

---

241. Judita govori Olofernu.

As I have told thee, nor repent I of it,
Tell me what I ask thee: for what cause
Didst thou leave the land to which I hasten,
    and come hither?"                                                       240
She approached him a bit closer, raised her eyes,
And spoke these words quietly in response to his words:[28]
"If a handmaid dare look into the eyes
Of her master, hear then my counsel;
For if the greatness of thy rule doth permit it,            245
It shall know what it desireth.
With thy help King Nabuchodonosor
Shall attain the whole world, not only this part of it,
And not only this city will serve him,
Thanks to thee, but all creation in season and out;       250
For word of thy bravery reacheth throughout all
    the world,
Of thy courage, power, perception and wisdom.
But let me tell thee of the madness of my people
Who do not give up their city to thy mercy:
They have angered God, Who by all the prophets       255
Hath warned them He will give them up to thee.
And because they know well their sin do they
    tremble in fear,
Turn laughter into tears, and torment themselves sighing;
Their bodies have grown lean, their visages pinched
    and sallow,
Their tongues coated with dust, racked with thirst,
    licking mud.                                                             260
They press the dregs from the livestock, wander around
Collecting it in their skirts, for their water is exhausted;
They have determined to slaughter their flocks
    with their young,
Lusting to drink their blood, however it might be,
Lusting to eat, they have resolved to use                   265
The vessels which have been consecrated,
In gold or gilt, for their own wine and grain,
And they will be polluted if these be so much as touched.
Do not doubt at all that they will perish for this,
They will die as surely as thou standest on this spot;      270
Thus I decided to flee and to come
Before thee to ask thee to give me safeguard.
Nor would this have been had our very own God
Who is in heaven not grown angry with them;

---

28. Judith answereth Holofernes.

275 »U griha bo barlog ne padoh s njimi ja,
»On ki je sam svemog, hoti da bižim tja
»I da navistim sva kâ će tako projti,
»Neka svitlost tvâ zna, jer jih će Bog ojti:
»Raba ću tva pojti jošće molit njega
280 »Da pravi dan dojti kad će raspa sega.
»Znan ćeš bit od svega kad se ja pomolim
»I tvoga posega spišen'je izmolim;
»Bude t' Jerosolim tvoj, dobro to ja znam,
»I s pukom oholim, Bog je to rekal nam.
285 »Tako da pakost vam u tom ne postane,
»Primajuć grad i hram, ni pas ne zalane:
»Da njih ovej rane navistim tebi tuj,
»Bog, ki nebom gane, posla ti rabu suj.
»A za tuj milost, kuj obitaš i stvoriš,
290 »Daj ti plaću onuj Bog koje dostojiš.
»Pravo je da stojiš slavan nada svimi,
»Da vazda zdrav hodiš i vesel s tvojimi.« —
Tako ričmi timi pokol mu vuhlova,
Kolinmi obimi poklek, skut celova:
295 Takoj ti svidova svinju, da utije,
Pomnja težakova, češuć oko šije;
Vode joj ulije i željudom pita,
Da ju pak ubije i dicu napita:
Ona hruča, rita, legne uz močiru,
300 Hvata iz korita; on oštri sikiru.
Vesel u svu mīru Oloferne tada,
Svim ričem da viru i ki stahu zada
Riše: »Mi do sada ne slišismo vide
»Od jezika mlada vetšije beside.
305 »Ot kuda iziđe ova jasna zora,
»Dostojna da side na nebesih zgora,
»Nabuk'donosora zovući: zemlju tuj
»Ostaviv i mora, hod ovdi gospoduj?
»Nî ti žene u svuj daržavu od svita,

---

293. Prilika.
303. Hvale lipost i razum Juditin.

For I have not fallen into the pit of sin with them, 275
He Who is omnipotent did decree that I flee
To reveal here all the things that will come to pass,
May thy majesty know that God will abandon them:
I, thy handmaid, shall also pray
That He tell me the day of their final destruction. 280
Thou shalt be known above all when I make my prayer
And win from Him the hastening of thy final victory;
Jerusalem shall be thine, this I know full well,
Together with its people, God hath told us so.
And no evil shall be done to thee in all this, 285
As thou takest town and temple, not even a dog
   will bark:
That I might announce to thee the wounds of this people,
God, who ruleth heaven, sent this thy handmaid to thee.
And for the mercy thou dost promise and do,
May God give thee the recompense that is thy due. 290
It is right that thou standest glorious above all,
That thou walkest in health and joy with thine own."
And when she had flattered him with these words,[29]
She knelt on both knees, and kissed the hem of his skirt:
Thus doth the peasant with great attentiveness 295
Care for the pig he fatteneth, and scratcheth it
   behind the ears,
Poureth it out water, and feedeth it rich food;
So that he might slaughter it, and give his children to eat:
It grunteth, it waddleth, it lieth against the mud wall,
It feedeth from the trough; he sharpeneth his ax. 300
Joyous beyond all measure Holofernes did believe
All these words, as did they standing near,
Who said:[30] "Till now we have never heard
Out of such a young mouth such sage old words.
Whence breaketh this bright dawn, 305
Worthy to be seated above in the heavens,
Who Summoneth Nabuchodonosor: Leave aside
Land and seas, and come reign here?
There is no such woman in all the realms of earth,

---

29. A comparison.
30. They praise Judith's beauty and wisdom.

310 »*Razum, lipost u kûj krasnije procvita;*
»*Ni kâ rič poskita slaje kad govori,*
»*Iz ust joj uresita kada jih otvori.*«
*Tako pod šatori veziri ki stahu*
*Govoreći, gori hvale nje dvizahu*
315 *I nju ti gledahu kâ prid Olofernom*
*Staše, gdi vijahu nju s Abrom nje vernom.*
»*Besidom bisernom*«, *Oloferne reče,*
»*I riču opernom sarce mi opteče:*
»*Sunce mi isteče Judita kad dojde;*
320 »*Onim ti odteče od kîhno ti pojde.*
»*Dobro da jih ojde, dobro Bog učini,*
»*Ki da ti vred projde k našim silam, čini,*
»*Veleći: svi ini ki su puka tvoga,*
»*Biti hoće plini skoro zbora moga.*
325 »*Obitan'ja toga ako se spuni stvar,*
»*Verovat ću Boga kîmno ti imaš mar;*
»*Biti će t' od nas har i parva čast u dvor,*
»*I taj će t' dati dar Nabukodonosor,*
»*Da ti ne bude par u mnozih gospoj hor.*«

---

317. Oloferne reče Juditi.

In whom reason, beauty, blossom more luxuriantly;                310
Nor who pronounceth more sweetly a word
With her lips when she openeth them."
Thus did the advisors who stood 'fore the tent
Praise her to the heavens with their speech,
And gaze upon her who was standing                               315
Before Holofernes, who looked at her and her
   faithful Abra.[31]
"With thy pearly speech," quoth Holofernes,
And thy winged words hast thou conquered my heart:
The sun did shine on me when Judith arrived,
And did set on them from whom she came.                          320
It was good that she left them, good that God did,
Who hath ordained that she should come to our armies,
Saying: all they of thy nation
Shall soon be captive to the multitude of my forces.
If this promise be fulfilled,                                    325
I too shall believe in this God whom thou dost worship;
We shall be grateful to thee, and give thee honour
   in our court,
And Nabuchodonosor shall reward thee in such a way
That thou shalt have no equal in the realm of
   many great ladies."

---

31. Holofernes speaketh to Judith.

## LIBRO PETO

    *Oloferne, pokol, tej riči zgovori,*
       *Tim, ki stahu okol, reče: »U komori,*
    *»Gdino su zatvori blagu sakrovitu*
    *»I tvardi, zapori povedte Juditu,*
5   *»Kâ po svojem svîtu, u kômno ni starvi,*
    *»Zemlju zlata situ dat nam će prez karvi;*
    *»Davajte joj parvi dil jistve i kruha,*
    *»Ki se meni marvi, kâ se meni kuha.«*
    *Judit strese uha: »Neću«, reče, »toga,*
10   *»Da ockvarniv duha, ne rasardim Boga;*
    *»Da jisti ću ovoga ča vo s sobom nosim,*
    *»Za da prî onoga, ča t' rekoh, isprosim;*
    *»I još da priprosim da spiši te strane*
       *»Dati t' Bog, ke mnozim po svitu su znane.«*
15     *On reče: »Tej hrane, ča ćeš učiniti,*
    *»Kada ti nestane, o čem ćeš živiti?«*
    *Ona se rotiti priča ponasmihnuv,*
       *Da brašno saspiti kô doni pribignuv*
       *Neće dokla dvignuv ruku svû ne svarši*
20     *I počine stignuv ča misal nje varšî.*
    *Baruni otparši vrata od ložišća,*
       *I svuda nastarši sviona krovišća,*
       *Rekoše: »Hladišća tuj su tvâ, gospoje.«*
       *Ona se namišća i reče: »Dobro je.«*
25   *Da parvo ovo je isprosila moleć,*
       *Molitve dit svoje u noći ishodeć;*
    *Da nitkor, odhodeć: »Kamo ćeš«, reče joj.*
    *Ni opet dohodeć: »Od kud greš? Ča je toj?«*
    *Toj biše dao njoj Oloferne, svojim*

---

    2. Kako Oloferne odredi stan Juditi osoba i dâ milost da u noći more ishoditi moliti Boga svoga.
    10. Da se ne ockvarni jidući ča biše branjeno u zakonu.

## Book The Fifth

After Holofernes had spoken these words,
To them that stood about him he said:[1] "To my chamber
Wherein are hoards of hidden goods
And mighty locks, lead Judith,
Who through her good counsel, containing no fraud,   5
Will deliver us bloodlessly a land filled with gold;
Give her the first choice of the meat and the bread
Which are prepared and served just for me."

Judith shook her head: "I shall not," quoth she,
"Anger God by profaning my spirit;[2]   10
For I shall eat only of what I have brought,
That I might ask for that of which I spoke to thee;
And also that I might ask God to hasten
Thy conquest of the lands known throughout the world."
He said: "What willst thou do,   15
When thy provision faileth thee, how willst thou live?"
Smiling she began to avere in reply
That she should not spend what she had brought in flight
Before she accomplish all by her own hand
And come to rest, having achieved what her mind had
    proposed.   20
His barons opened the gates of her sleeping chamber
And spread over all coverlets of silk,
Saying: "Here, my lady, are thy chambers."
She, taking her place, said: "This will do."
But first she did ask their permission   25
To go forth at night unto prayer;
That none, as she leave, say to her: "Whither goest?"
Nor upon her return might they ask: "Whence? What for?"
This Holofernes granted her, and to his guards

---

1. How Holofernes did set apart an apartment for Judith and graciously allow her to go out at night to pray to her God.
2. Lest she pollute herself by eating what was forbidden in the law.

30         *Vratarom tad takoj zapovid čine' svim:*
*Taj slobod dvima njim, Abri ter Juditi,*
*Da bude, ne inim, za tri dni služiti.*
*Ona ishoditi jâ k drâge slazeći,*
*K potoku hoditi vodom se čisteći;*
35         *A pak uzlazeći Bogu se moljaše,*
*Da, puk slobodeći, spuni ča mišljaše.*
*Zatim čista staše u komoru došad,*
*Ni se okusaše ner jur sunce zapad;*
*Kô četvartom izšad, svitlost svim ljudem dâ,*
40         *I Oloferne tad dvor na večeru zva.*
*Slugu Vagava sla da Juditi veli*
*Da sram odvarže tja, da se k njemu seli*
*I ča on uzveli, pristane učinit,*
*A dar, kîno želi, svaki hoće imit;*
45         *Jer mu će prirok bit da žena stoji tuj,*
*A on da će živit želeć imiti njuj. —*
*Pojde Vagav i suj besidu poni njoj.*
*»Vladiko«, reče, »v onuj jure komoru poj*
*»Gdino gospodin moj sedeći počiva,*
50         *»Želeći obraz tvoj ki suncu odsiva:*
*»Zatoj te priziva da s njim i piješ i jiš,*
*»Da vesel pribiva dokol uza nj sidiš.«*
*»Kâ sam ja da barž mniš,« Judit odgovori,*
*»Da neću na pospiš pojt u toj komori?*
55         *»Ki su moji opori, da hizat uz ostan*
*»Mogu, ali gori reć: Niže mene stân?*
*»Bud poni dobro znan, ča je drago njemu:*
*»Meni je kako man i slatko u svemu;*
*»Raba ću bit temu za moga života,*
60         *Ako mu sam čemu zna njega dobrota.«*
*Takoj riči mota Judita vesela,*
*Da je ta pohota Oloferna svela*
*Na taka jur mela da će leći nice,*

---

39. **Kako Oloferne četvarti dan zva Juditu hoteći da s njim pribiva.**
47. **Vagav, vratar Olofernov.**
53. **Odgovori Judit Vagavu.**

Gave he the following command: 30
To the two of them, Abra and Judith, this license
Be given, not to others, to hold for three days.
She began to go out and down to a dell,
To a fountain of water where she washed;
And coming out again, she prayed to God, 35
That freeing her people, He fulfill her intention.
Then she returned, having been made clean, to her tent,
Nor did she taste her meat until the sun set;
When it rose the fourth time, giving light to all people,[3]
Holofernes summoned all his court to a feast. 40
He sent his servant Bagoas to order Judith
To cast off her shame and come to his chambers,
And to agree to do whatever he might command,
And any gift she might desire she would surely have;
For it was a reproach to him that a woman be present 45
Whom he desired but lived on without her.
Bagoas[4] went and took these words to her:
"My lady," quoth he, "go then to that tent
Wherein my lord doth lie at his rest
And doth wish to see thy visage which reflecteth the sun: 50
Thus doth he summon thee to eat and drink with him,
That he might be merry with thee at his side."
"Who am I," saith Judith,[5] "to gainsay thee,
That I will not hasten to go to his chambers?
What power have I in me to kick against the goad, 55
Or to say to this mountain: stand lower than I?
For I know full well what is dear to him,
And this is my manna, and sweetness above all;
I shall be his handmaiden all the days of my life,
If in his goodness he find some use in me." 60
Such words spake Judith in her joy
For that lust had already brought Holofernes
Into such dangerous waters that he might succumb,

---

3. How Holofernes on the fourth day did summon Judith, desiring that she should tarry with him.
4. Bagoas, Holofernes' steward.
5. Judith answereth Bagoas.

          A gradi i sela steći parvo lice.
65    Kad spusti udice ter zadije ribu,
          I stežuć tunjice, mahne gori šibu
          Ribar i potribu ima jur dat ju van,
          Radostan da hlibu smok mu je pripravan:
          Tako, kad osnovan jur misli svoje teg
70       Vidi Judit, izvan urehe na se usteg
          I skuta pouspreg, radosna pojde tad,
          Da tuj, rukom poseg, osnovu otka sad.
          Oloferne nju kad prid sobom ugleda,
          U ljubavi zašad, sarce mu uspreda;
75       Slaja mu bî meda, da gorkost će žerat,
          Studeniji leda kada bude ležat.
          Kon sebe ju pojat hiti za tarpezom
          I niže njeje stat zapovidi knezom;
          Njoj reče: »Obezom jesi me obezala,
80       »Jer harlim potezom dojti si hajala.
          »Tim si dostojala da pri mni milosti,
          »Kû želiš, imala budeš u radosti;
          »Sad vesela dosti sa mnom pij ter blaguj
          »I s ovimi gosti obilo se počtuj.«
85    Ona njemu uz tuj zahvalivši, reče:
          »Veselo ću stvar tuj učinit, jer steče
          »Blagost, pokol čeče uza te raba tvâ,
          »Kâ želiš da kleče prida te zemlja sva.«
          Tad pi i blagova ča biše opravila
90       Abra i gotova prida nju stavila.
          Mev tim je nudila njega da ji i pije,
          Ter ga veselila da se većma nalije;
          Da kada se opije, zaspi i zahrope,
          Požre takoj osje, da veće ne sope. —
95       O, kîno se tope u žartju mnogomu,
          Vijte kako ope život sad ovomu!

---

    65. Prilika.
    79. Govori Oloferne Juditi, posadiv ju kon sebe za večerom.
    85. Odgovara Judit.
    95. Govoren'je protiv zalihu žartju i pitju.

And the cities and towns regain their former aspect.
When he casteth his rod and catcheth a fish,⁶     65
And letting out his line, jerketh back his pole,
The fisherman hath need to draw the fish out,
Rejoicing that a condiment hath been furnished for
   his bread,
So too Judith, seeing the web of her plan well cast,
Did deck herself outwardly     70
And spreading her skirts, joyously go thither
So that, at her touch, the net be woven tighter still.
When Holofernes caught sight of her before him,
He fell in love, and his heart was enflamed;
Sweeter was she to him than honey, though he would taste     75
Bitterness when he lay colder than ice.
He hastened to seat her by his side at the table,
And his princes he ordered to sit beneath her.
To her he said:⁷ "Thou hast bound me with thy bindings,
For that thou hast cared to hasten to my side.     80
Thereby hast thou merited to gain from me the grace
Thou desirest, and that in full joy;
Now, o happy one, eat and drink with me to thy fill,
And make merry in full measure with these my guests."
Thanking him she said in reply:⁸     85
"Joyously shall I do this thing, for thy handmaiden
Winneth thine indulgence as she sitteth at thy side
And desireth that all the lands be prostrate 'fore thee."
Then ate and drank she what Abra had prepared
And placed now in readiness before her.     90
At the same time she urged him to eat and drink,
And entertained him that he should pour all the more;
So that when he became drunk, he should snooze
   and snore,
And swallow the hook, that he breathe no more.
O ye who wallow in gluttonous sin,⁹     95
See how Holofernes' life now fleeth from him!

---

6. A comparison.
7. Holofernes addresseth Judith, having placed her next to himself at the supper table.
8. Judith respondeth.
9. An address against excessive eating and drinking.

>     Na njemu samomu grih je tâ naudil,
>     Da jošće svakomu u kom je kada bil.
>     S toga je izgubil Adam s Evom milost,
> 100 Kû je najpri jimil, svih vargši u žalost.
>     Noe svoju sramost otkrivši grubo spa,
>     Kad ga obali jakost vina kô garlu dâ.
>     Lota kad pijanost jâ, ne znajuć spi uz kih,
>     Mâ njih, kim biše ćâ, čini sinov svojih.
> 105 Esav liše tih parvorojen'ja čast
>     I blagoslovi svih očevih zgubi slast;
>     Jer davši garlu vlast pri voli požriti
>     Od zdile jedne mast ner sve to imiti.
>     Puk božji živiti o pići nebeskoj
> 110 Počan, jâ marziti, objistan jur, na toj;
>     Egipskih lonac loj želeći, ushvali,
>     I njih mnozih zatoj Bog smartno popali.
>     Običaj on zali sinov Hele popa,
>     Ki su umicali meso iz ukropa,
> 115 Smartju jih pokopa, vze njemu popovstvo,
>     Jer ne poja štropa na njih nepodopstvo.
>     Vino ter oholstvo Aleksandra smami
>     Tako da ubojstvo svojimi rukami
>     Stvori, pak suzami lica gorko umi
> 120 Obujat tugami: toko draga ubi.

---

101. Noe opi se i zaspa otkriven. Kama sina prokle, jer se naruga; Sema i Jafeta blagoslovi, ki ga pokriše.

104. Lota hćere opojiše, s pijanim spaše i rodiše: starija rodi Moaba, od koga bi narod od Moabiti; mlaja rodi Amona, od koga bi narod od Amoniti. Zato di: oni kim biše ćâ, a to otac, učini jih mâ, a to matere svojih sinov.

105. Esav za zdilu leće proda prav pravorojen'ja svoga bratu Jakobu. Tim izgubi očev blagoslov.

112. Ovo bi, kad od Egipta diliv se, gredihu pustinjom s Mojsesom.

115. Sini Hele popa umicahu meso onim ki činjahu posvetilišća. Cić toga biše ubijeni od neprijatelj, a od njegove kuće veće ne bi pop, jer jih ne pokara, kako imaše.

120. Aleksandar pijan ubi Klita, baruna svoga. Kada se razabra jutridan, ja pitati gdi je Klit, i od žalosti ne htiše jisti, hteći i sam umriti, da ini ga pripraviše.

Nor was he alone ensnared by this vice,
But each and everyone who e'er partook of it.
For this reason did Adam and Eve lose the grace
That formerly they enjoyed, casting all into grief.              100
Noah grossly slept having shown his nakedness,[10]
When the force of the wine he drunk o'ertook him.
Lot, the captive of drink, knew not with whom he slept,
And made of those he fathered the mothers of his sons.[11]
Esau was deprived of the honour of first birth[12]              105
And the sweetness of his father's blessings;
For giving his gullet power he prefered to consume
The meat of one stewpot than to have all the rest.
The People of God, accustomed to eating heavenly food,
Grew to hate it when they had eaten their fill;                 110
They began to praise the fleshpots of Egypt and
    desire them,
So that God consumed many of them in His fiery wrath.[13]
He disapproved the way of priest Elias' sons,
Who did steal the meat from out of the soup:
He dealt them death, removed his priestly rank,[14]             115
For he had failed to scourge their indecencies.
Wine and arrogance did Alexander entice
So that he commited murder with his own hands,
Then washed his face in bitter tears,
So bound about with grief for having slain his friend.[15]      120

---

10. Noah was drunk and fell asleep exposed. He cursed his son Ham, who did deride him; Shem and Japheth he did bless, for they covered him.
11. Lot's daughters made him drunk, slept with him and gave birth: the elder to Moab, from whom the Moabite race did spring; the younger to Ammon, from whom the Ammonite race did spring. Therefore he saith: "And made of those he fathered the mothers of his sons." (Marulić explains in the verse he cites his use of "čâ" for father [otac] and "mâ" for mothers [matere]–HC.)
12. Esau for a mess of pottage did sell the right of the first born to his brother Jacob. Thus did he lose his father's blessing.
13. This was after they had departed from Egypt and were walking through the desert with Moses.
14. The sons of Eli the priest did rob the meat of them who made sacrifices. For that they were slain by the enemy, and of his household he was no longer priest, for he had not chastised them as he ought.
15. Alexander when drunk did slay Clitus, his captain. When on the following day he regained his senses, he began to inquire where Clitus be, and from grief he would not eat, desiring only that he himself die, but others did prevent him.

Centaure pogubi Peritov s Lafiti,
Jer hvataje zubi, jur pijani i siti,
Onih kih počtiti njih dostojaše se,
Za žene zaditi ne sramovaše se.
125 Saki zgubiše se kad u Cirov okol
Stupiv, objiše se, opiše; i pokol
Legoše kako vol, on na nje napusti,
Razbil jih, dâ jim bol, živih jih ne pusti.
Vino život shusti Lacida i Krisipa,
130 Mudrost od njih usti začarni taj sipa;
Taj konac opipa pitanski Arceslav,
I on pijan udipa u Karonovu plav.
Toj se hudinji dav Antiok, moguć kralj,
Jaki kakono lav, s kîmi je za sto stal,
135 Bî jih pijan; bî njim žal; tarpiti ne htiše
Sramotu i pečal ter ti ga ubiše.
Bolje ti mu biše u boj smart prijati,
Još kada imiše sa Rimnjani rati,
Nere živu stati do stotin lit roka
140 Pak konac imati tolika priroka.
Raskoša obroka i vina kô sarka
Učini žestoka Antonija Marka:

---

124. Centaure, ki s njim mejašahu, zva na svoj pir Peritov, kralj od Lafiti; oni objivši se i opivši pohitiše za žene: zato jih pobi.
128. Saki jest bio niki narod u Persiju: kîh budući vojska mnoga, kralj Cir od Persije čini se bižati ter jim pusti okol pun vina i brašna svakoga; oni sedoše tuj piti i jisti. Kad biše puni, razlegoše se: on na nje pripusti i pobi jih.
131. Lacid, Krisip, Arceslav: toj su bili naučeni filozofi, da garlu se daše. Niki, diju, umri vino pijući, a niki cić toga u tarpju, upadši pogibe.
132. Karon je ki brodi duše u paklu, kako diju poeti.
136. Antiok, kralj od Sirije, ki Rimnjanom rat čini, pijan bi svojih, a oni ga ubiše.
142. Marko Antonij velik biše žarlac i opijavac; pobi vele grajan, polaču vlastelina jednoga darova kuhaču svomu, jer mu biše ugodno skuhao. Pijan u viće bljuva. Obljubi Kleopatru, kraljicu od Aleksandrije, a ženu pusti, kâ biše sestra Oktavijana cesara, i s toga pogibe.

Piritheus of the Laphits the Centaurs did slay,
For grinding their teeth, full of drink and meat,
They did not forbear to pursue the wives
Of them who had deigned invite them to a feast.[16]
The Sakis did perish when they entered Cyrus' camp    125
And ate and drank their fill; they lay
Like oxen, till he did attack them,
Smash them, inflicting much pain, nor did
   he let them live.[17]
Wine did ruin the lives of Lacidus and Chrysippus,
Pouring did darken the wisdom of their mouths;    130
The same end did Archesilaeus encounter of Pitany:[18]
Drunken he lept into Charon's bark.[19]
Of like ignominy did Antiochus, mighty king, partake,
Strong as a lion, besotted he struck at his guests at table.
They took pity: but unwilling to bear    135
The shame and the sorrow, they did slay him.[20]
It would have been better for him to die in battle
Whilst he made war on the Romans,
Than to live to his hundredth year
And find such a shameful end.    140
Sumptuous dinners and the wine he embibed
Rendered Marc Anthony very cruel:[21]

---

16. . The Centaurs, who did border with him, were summoned to a feast by Piritheus, King of the Laphits; having eaten and drunk to excess, they pursued the Laphit women; therefore he did slay them.
17. The Sakis were a nation in Persia: their army being large, King Cyrus of Persia pretended to flee but left behind for them a camp full of wine and meal of all sorts; they sat down to drink and eat. When they were sated, they stretched out: he fell upon them and slew them.
18. Lacidus, Chrysippus, Archesilaeus: these were learned philosophers who did indulge their gullets. One, it is said, died whilst drinking wine, and another, for the same reason, did in agony fall down dead.
19. Charon is he who ferrieth souls to hell, as the poets say.
20. Antiochus, King of Syria, who made war upon the Romans, was made drunk by his own men, who did slay him.
21. Marc Anthony was a great glutton and drunkard; he slew many citizens, he gave the palace of a nobleman to his cook for he had cooked well for him. Drunk, he vomited before his counsellors. He fell in love with Cleopatra, the Queen of Alexandria, and divorced his wife, who was the Emperor Octavian's sister, and perished as a result.

   Silan po Rim tarka vlastele koljući,
   Njih blago rastarka kuhačem dajući.
145 Toj ga potičući Kleopatru ljubi,
   Ženu pušćujući; po tom sebe zgubi.
   Ki su taki zubi, zlobe će nadvrići,
   Kako vethe rubi kripost će odvrići;
   Na konac nesrići upast će u svakoj:
150 Nemoć jih će sići, štumak ne dat pokoj,
   Smalit će razbor svoj i jošće iman'je,
   Pak u vikomnji znoj biti će njih stan'je,
   Zadit će smijan'je drugi, rič sû čuvši,
   Govorit: zaman je, tarbuh nima uši,
155 Razbire piću ši i slasti privraća,
   I vina okuši, ter u se sve svraća.
   Da kino se odvraća od dobra nauka,
   Prida nj se ne izvraća ča se totu kljuka;
   Tim piše mâ ruka, kîmno svetu duhu
160 Ne zgodit jest muka veća ner tarbuhu;
   Ki nimaju buhu huda utvarjen'ja,
   Zalizlu u uhu spasena slišen'ja.
   Da jur govoren'ja rič se tamo vrati,
   Na saj spoviden'ja otkle se uvrati.
165 Oloferne stati na noge prejedva
   Mogaše; jer jati koko mogahu dva,
   Toliko sam on z'žva i obuja ga san.
   Vagav zatvaruć, zva inih da gredu van.
   Idoše na svoj stan, sobom teturaje',
170 Jerbo ne jedan žban popiše spijaje':
   Redom začinjaje', zdravicu obnose',
   Jednu popijaje', a drugu donose'.
   Pojdoše zanose' tud ovud nogami,
   Sami se nadnose, kimljući glavami;
175 U obraz jim plami a na nosu para,
   I na brade prami lašćaše se ckvara.
   Tarbuh kako žara nadmen odstojaše,

---

147. Koliko zlo dohodi cića garla.
163. Vraća na počitan'je historije govoren'je.
173. Kako pijani gredihu ki se čtovaše s Holofernom.

Racing about Rome in his power he did empale the nobles,
Carry off their wealth and distribute it to his cooks.
Stimulated by this, he was smitten by Cleopatra 145
And left his own wife; thus brought he on his own ruin.
They who are so greedy will heap up ill-fortune;[22]
Like so much old clothing, they cast off their strength;
At the end they will fall into every misfortune:
Their weakness will undercut them, their belly give
    them no peace, 150
Their sense will be diminished and with it their wealth,
And their final state will be eternal fire.
Another, hearing these words, will surely laugh,
And reply: 'tis all in vain, the belly hath no ears,
It selecteth its food and digesteth its delights; 155
It sampleth wine and fitteth all things in.
But he who doth turn from goodly counsel
Doth not perceive what here is laid out:
My hand doth write for them who are more loath
Not to please the Holy Ghost than their own bellies; 160
For them whose ears a flea of wicked stubborness
Hath not blocked to salvific listening.
Now let the thread of narration turn thither[23]
Whence it hath distanced itself for the sake of this advice.

Holofernes was barely able to stand 165
On his feet, for as much as two could eat,
So much had he consumed and sleep did overtake him.
Bagoas closed the tent and ordered the others to leave,
They made their way tottering to their tents,
For they had drunk not one jug in a draught: 170
Making up songs, they drank toast after toast,
No sooner finishing one than another was brought.
Their legs all akimbo, they made many a false start,[24]
Waving their heads and tripping o'er each other;
Their faces were aflame, and fumes were at their noses, 175
And grease did glisten on the hairs of their chins.
Their bellies peeked out, swollen like a pot;

---

22. How much evil doth proceed from the gullet.
23. The address returneth to the narration of the history.
24. How they who paid their respects to Holofernes did walk drunk.

Rič, kû potopara, jazik prikošaše;
Sviste ne saznaše, ctakljahu jim oči,
180 Rugo njimi staše i smih se potoči;
Jer niki o ploči udri sobom pad se,
Niki se pomoči, niki kara svad se,
Niki daržat rad se, druga uhitiše,
Ter i s drugom zad se uznak uzvarziše;
185 A niki rigniše, niki se gnušahu,
A niki ležiše, niki na nj padahu;
A druzih nošahu, stavit jih na odar:
Toko se saznahu koko martav tovar.
Tko će imiti var ustegnuti garla,
190 Pogledaj ovi bar ter vij je l' umarla
Tuj čast i doparla tamnost i gardinja,
Kâ je oto svarzla da je vitez svinja.
Sad vij kako linja Olofernja sila,
Kako ju raščinja hot nečista dila. —
195 Postilja je bila na sridu komori,
Mehka, čista, bila, s pisani zastori.
Na njoj se obori Oloferne unid,
Zaspa većma gori nego morski medvid;
Spući ga tako vid' Judit, Abri svojoj
200 »Poj polako naprid,« reče, »na vratih stoj!«
Ove dvi tad u toj ložnici ostale
S Olofernom, u njoj ne bihu zaspale;
Poni od tej stale na vratoh Abra sta,
Jesu l' straže pale, oslihovati jâ.
205 I straže i čeljad sva kâ biše okoli,
Biše kako martva; svi bo na tom stoli
Jiše kako voli, da još veće piše:
Bditi ne bi koli, straže ne činiše.
Ki je nebes više i ki svaka more,
210 Jur odlučil biše puku da pomore. —
Judita zastore postilji razmače,
Sarce joj kopore', bliže se primače.
Ruku s rukom stače i k nebu podvignu,

---

197. Oloferne zaspa.

Their tongues cut off any word they might let slip;
They lost their reason; their eyes were all glassy,
They behaved most shamelessly, and were smitten
    with laughter;                                             180
For one had crashed against a board in his fall,
Another pissed, still others did argue and quarrel.
To hold themselves up, one grabbed onto another,
And both fell down and landed on their backs.
Some vomited, others grew nauseated,               185
Some lay on the ground, others fell on them;
Still others had to be carried to their beds:
They had as much sense as a dead donkey.
He who is able to refrain from greedy thoughts
Should regard these people to see if indeed         190
Honour hath died and wicked sinfulness replaced it,
The which turneth a noble into a swine.
See how Holofernes' strength doth melt away,
How the filthy deeds of lust dilute it.
The bed was in the middle of the chamber,       195
Soft, clean, white, with silken curtains.
Entering, Holofernes collapsed upon it,[25]
He began to snore louder than a sea lion;
Seeing him thus asleep, Judith said to her Abra,
"Walk ahead of me slowly, and stand at the door!"    200
The two of them had remained in that chamber
With Holofernes; nor had they fallen asleep;
Then did Abra go to stand at the door,
And began to listen for the quieted guard.
The guard and the servants and all round about     205
Were like the dead; for all had at that table
Eaten like oxen and drunk even more:
To watch there was no one, and none to stand guard.
He Who is higher than the heavens, and can do
    all things,
Had already decided to help His own people.         210
Judith moved aside the curtains of the bed,
Whilst her heart beat fiercely, she moved closer to it.
She joined hand to hand and raised both to heaven,

---

25. Holofernes falleth asleep.

|     | Na kolina klače i suzami rignu; |
| --- | --- |
| 215 | Glasa ne izdvignu, da moli u sebi: |

»Bože, daj da stignu ča je godi tebi;
»Stvori milost meni, pokrip rabu tvoju,
»Strah mi vas odnemi, dvigni ruku moju
»Da stvar svarši koju misal moja plodi,
220  »Da se tebe boju puci ter narodi!
»Sada, sada hodi, tvoj grad Jerosolim
»Od nevolj slobodi i vas puk tvoj, molim;
»Rasap daj oholim ki se uzvišuju,
»Pokoj pošlji boljim ki se ponižuju.
225 »Ovo ča veruju po tebi ja moći,
»Koko potribuju, hotij mi pomoći,
»U dne ter u noći tebi da hvalu dam,
»Jer u tvoje moći sad svaršit to uzdam.«
   To rekši dviže ram i na nogah postup,
230   Ter muče bičag snam ki višaše o stup,
   Podri ga, kič mu zdup Oloferna jednom,
   A drugom rukom lup kla, skube objednom.
   Hronu, strepi sobom, ležeći on uznak,
   Darhta ruka s nogom, vas se oslabi, pak
235  Izdaše; ne bi jak; garkljanom siča karv:
   Tako t' zgibe junak, tako spusti obarv.
   Zgrize ga mao čarv oružjem njegovim,
   Ubi ga ženska sarv, ki biše prostro dim
   Da zajme svitom svim; ki mnjaše da ni Bog
240  Silam njegovim tim jest protiviti mog.
   Prostri se tuj nebog, prez glave, kako panj,
   Juditi Bog pomog kada napade na nj;
   Da joj ni trud zamanj, da stvari viru dâ,
   Prikla ga, steć uza nj i odni glavu tja.
245 I Abri reče: »Nâ, u dvanjke toj zatvor!«
   Sama se prope i sta, skide s odra nastor;
   Odvaliv trup odzgor, pak po običaj svoj

---

216. Molitva Judite kad hoti ubiti Oloferna.
229. Kako ga ubi jednom rukom za vlase uhitiv ga, a drugom koljući.
238. Sarv: sarvan'je.

She fell to her knees and poured forth tears;
She did not raise her voice, but prayed to herself:[26]  215
"O God, allow me to do what pleaseth Thee;
Be merciful unto me, strengthen Thy handmaiden,
Remove from me all fear, guide my arm
That it accomplish that which my mind hath plotted,
That all nations and peoples might fear Thee!  220
Now, now, I pray, free Thy city Jerusalem
From bondage and liberate all Thy people;
Smite the arrogant who elevate themselves,
Give peace to the virtuous who humble themselves.
What I believe give me Thy power to do  225
As it be necessary, and deign to assist me,
Night or day that I might render Thee praise,
For I trust in Thy might to accomplish this."
This she said, then straightened her shoulders and stood,[27]
Silently she took the sword from the pillar of the bed,  230
And drew it: with one hand she seized Holofernes' hair,
With the other smote him, swiftly pulling the blade.
He groaned, shuddered, lying on his back,
His arm and leg twitched, went weak, and then
He expired; he had no strength; from his throat
   dribbled blood:  235
Thus the hero perished, thus closed he his eyes.
A tiny worm bit him with his own sword,
A woman conquered[28] him who once had boasted
He would take the whole world; who thought not
   e'en God
Would be able to resist his mighty forces.  240
He lay here stretched out, wretch, like a log,
God did help Judith when she fell upon him;
That her work be not in vain, to give weight to her
   words,
Standing beside him she smote again and took off
   his head.
She said to Abra: "Here, put this in our bags!"  245
She herself stood up, pulled the cover from the bed,
Dragging the body down with it; then as was their wont

---

26. Judith's prayer as she resolveth to slay Holofernes.
27. How she slew him, seizing him with one hand by the hair, and with the other stabbing.
28. "Conquered": overpowering. (Marulić explains Croatian "sarv," conquest, with "sarvan'je," conquering–HC.)

    *Izidoše na dvor, kako da mole ophoj.*
    *Ne dav nogam pokoj, projdoše vas okol,*
250  *Prem da jim biše znoj, obvargoše prodol.*
    *Kako kada sokol uhvati lovinu,*
    *Zavije se više školj, side na visinu,*
    *Ne pustiv živinu iz nohat, kû je jal,*
    *Dokla dopre stinu gdi je gnjizdo svijal;*
255  *Harlo ti je lital, da se napitaju*
    *Ptići, jerbo je znal da lačni čekaju:*
    *Tako t' ne sustaju ove dvi, ni sidu,*
    *Dokla ugledaju vahtare na zidu;*
    *Pojdoše po brigu, i kad bi blizu vrât,*
260  *Judita napridu uzupi, napan vrât:*
    *»Otvorte, otvorte grad, jere je s nami Bog,*
    *»Otvorte, otvorte; sad on ki je svemog*
    *»Puku svomu pomog, skazal je svu kripost,*
    *»Nečistih u barlog varže, nâm dâ milost.«*
265  *Prijam jih u naglost, stražane idoše,*
    *Nenadinu radost tu popom rekoše,*
    *I svi se stekoše, Juditu vidiše,*
    *Svitil'ja snesoše, jerbo još noć biše.*
    *Judita sta više i jer staše gromor, —*
270  *Svi bo se čudiše, ne mneći jur nitkor*
    *Da ju on sčeka zbor — rukom dâ zlamen'ja,*
    *Da muče ter govor sliše, nje činjen'ja.*
    *Uši na slišan'ja dvigoše primuknuv;*
    *Reče: »Umiljen'ja pridajte poniknuv*
275  *»Bogu, jer uzdvignuv on ki u nj ufaju,*
    *»Onih bî prikinuv kîno ga ne haju.*
    *»Kîno toku vaju nas pridati napi,*
    *»Karvi tuje žaju, svoju pivši, zapi;*
    *»Glas vaš Boga vapi, i Bog rukom mojom,*
280  *»Oloferna skvapi sû noć pravdom svojom.«*
    *Tad pohvativ rukom 'z dvanjak ize glavu,*
    *Ukaza prid pukom strašnu, svu karvavu,*
    *Klanu kako bravu. »Evo glava«, reče,*

---

251. Prilika.
274. Govori Judita puku prišad u grad, ubiv Oloferna.

They went out into the courtyard, as if to pray.
Nor gave they their feet rest till they had crossed
   the camp,
Though sweat covered them, they went 'round the valley.   250
As when the hawk seizeth his prey,[29]
He soareth above the crags, and sitteth on the peak,
Nor letteth he the prey go from his clenching talons
Till he reach the cliff wherein his nest is woven,
Hastily he flieth, so that his chicks may eat   255
For he knoweth that they await him enhungered:
So these two women, who neither pause nor sit,
Till they catch sight of the watchmen on the walls;
They went along the embankment, and right by the gates,
Judith raised her head and cried out before her:   260
"Open, open the fortress, for God is with us,
Open, open: for He who is omnipotent
Hath holpen His people, shown all His might,
Cast down the impious, and given us grace."
Letting them in quickly, the guards did run   265
To announce this unexpected joy to the priests,
And all came together, and they saw Judith,
And they brought lamps, for it was still night.
Judith stood above them, for there was a din–
All were amazed, in that none had thought   270
Such a crowd would greet her–and she signaled with
   her hand
That they grow silent and listen to the tale of her deeds.
They pricked their ears and listened in silence;
She said:[30] "Repent and bow before God,
For He raiseth them who trust in Him,   275
And smitteth them who worship Him not.
He who sought to bring us to such great grief,
Thirsty for others' blood, has drinking quaffed his own;
Your voice cried out to God, and God by my hand
Hath this night in His justice laid hold of Holofernes."   280
Then waving she drew from her bags the head,
Showed it to the people, all bloody and horrid,
Sliced off like a gelding. "Behold the head," she said,

---

29. A comparison.
30. Judith addresseth the people, having returned to the city after killing Holofernes.

»*Kâno sù daržavu priti da rasteče.*«
285 Pak razvivši peče: »*Evo,*« reče, »*karzan,*
»*Na kom pjan pričeče, na kom karvju parzan*
»*Osta vele marzan, kad od jedne žene*
»*Smartju bi povarzan, Bog pomogši mene,*
»*Ki stvar tako rene, ki moga počten'ja*
290 »*Čuva da ne uvene s nikoga zgrišen'ja;*
»*Dâ meni vraćen'ja, dâ sebi dobitje,*
»*Dâ vam slobojen'ja dâ svim dobro žitje.*
»*Njemu poni pitje slavno htijmo peti,*
»*Tere žgati žartje, a zlobe odneti,*
295 »*Pravoga oteti: to će biti dike*
»*Njemu, ki je sveti, milostiv u vike.*«
Vidivši puk like nevolj svojih, pokol
Bog jur protivnike smete i njih okol,
Prignuše glavu dol, njemu zahvališe
300 Slaveć njegov pristol, Juditu hvališe.
Ozija tuj biše, od veselja suzi,
Radosno uzdiše videć konac tuzi.
Kakono ki upuzi u porat jur mneći,
Da ga val pogruzi — vitar strašno dmeći —
305 Raduje se steći zgibil koj ubiže,
U sebi misleći, ter spasan kû stiže:
Hvalu Bogu dviže da ga ne poklopi
More i ne stiže, kô mnozih potopi:
Tako ti mev popi vesel Ozija stav,
310 Sû besidu sklopi: »*Boga svak*«, reče, »*slav!*
»*Ki milo k nam ustav, i moć ženske desne*
»*Moćju svojom nadav, protivnim glavu sne.*
»*U noći ter u dne budi vazda s nami;*
»*Pečal, misli trudne vazda nam odnami,*
315 »*A ti mev ženami blažena s' Judita,*
»*Blažen Bog ki rami svojimi te šćita,*
»*I od zla zamita, i ruku upravi*
»*Na smart koga prita vas svit u strah stavi;*

---

301. Kako se Ozija obeseli.
303. Prilika.
310. Govori Ozija puku i Juditi:

"Which had threatened to destroy our land."
Then unfolding the cloth she said: "Behold the pelt             285
On which he lay drunk, on which, blood bespattered,
He grew very cold when, by one woman,
He was crushed to death, for God helped me,
Who did direct the matter and preserve my honour
That it not be tainted by any sin;                               290
He granted me safe return, granted Himself the victory,
Granted you freedom and granted all a good life.
To Him then let us sing our song of praise
And make sacrifice, drive out all evil
And redeem the righteous; all to the glory                       295
Of Him Who is holy and merciful forever."
The people perceiving the balm for their woes,
As God scattered their enemy and his camp,
Bowed low their heads and gave Him thanks,
Glorifying His throne and praising Judith.                       300
Ozias was here, weeping in his joy,[31]
He sighed happily seeing an end to their woes.
Like one who reacheth a harbour still thinking[32]
That a wave will o'ertake him–the wind bloweth
 fearsomely–
He rejoiceth as he pondereth the ruin he hath 'scaped,           305
And the safety toward which he saileth;
He praiseth God for that the wave doth not cover him,
Nor the sea reach him, though it hath drowned many:
So Ozias, rejoicing midst the priests,
Composed these words:[33] "Each man praise God!                  310
Who hath been merciful to us, and the might of
 a woman's arm,
Supplemented by His own, did remove our foe's head;
May He be both day and night ever with us;
Sorrow, bitter thoughts may He drive far from us,
And blessed, Judith, art thou among women,                       315
Blessed is God Whose shoulders do shield thee,
Who protecteth thee from evil, guideth thy hand
To slay him whose threats did terrify the whole world;

---

31. How Ozias did rejoice.
32. A comparison.
33. Ozias addresseth Judith and the people.

>»Tako te proslavi, da će t' hvale dati,
320  »U svita daržavi svi ki budu stati.
     »Prî će se vraćati ka vrilu vode rik,
     »Po moru plavati od svih težina sik,
     »Svitlost sunčenih zrik u istok zahodit,
     »Nere će tvojih dik slavan glas ne hodit,
325  »Kâ život ohodit nisi se šćedila,
     »Za ovi slobodit puk od pogibila;
     »Platit takaj dila nitkor nas ne more,
     »Božja t' jih plat sila, kâno svaka more.«
     Toj on dogovore, ki bihu tuj ljudi,
330  Svi usta rastvore, riše: »Tako budi!« —
     Dozvan dojde tudi i Akior nebog,
     Pače blag, kad trudi olahča mu nalog.
     Reče mu Judit: »Bog izraelski danas,
     »Koga, da je uzmog obarovati nas,
335  »Ti reče, neka znaš, prilika u ruku mû
     »Vrat, kako jedan vlas, neverniku tomu;
     »A da vidiš komu, ovo t' glava onoga,
     »U oholstvu svomu ki pogardi Boga,
     »A tebe dilj toga reče da će zgubit,
340  »Kad puka ovoga klat bude i rubit.«
     Akior u subit prenu se, ugledav
     Glavu kâ ga ubit reče, totu zagnav;
     I ništar ne postav, pristrašen poniknu,
     Kako na koga lav iznevarke riknu.
345  Kad se dviže, kleknu polag njeje nogu,
     Pokloniv se, reknu: »Blažena s' pri Bogu,
     »Bogu tvom, ki mnogu svim po te milost dâ;
     »Moć njega svemogu hvaliti će svuda
     »Po svem svita stogu, sluti budeš kuda.«

---

341. Kako se Akior pristraši ugledav glavu Olofernu i prija viru židovsku i pribiva u Betuliju do smarti s obitil'ju svojom, videći moć Boga izraelskoga.

May He glorify thee that all speak of thy praise
Who henceforth forever live in this world.     320
Sooner shall the rivers return to their sources,
The weight of the mountains float on the sea,
The brightness of the sun set in the east,
Than the sound of thy praises pass away,
Thou didst not hesitate to leave this life,     325
In order to save this people from destruction;
None of us can ever recompense these deeds,
May God's power, which can do all, repay thee."
When he had said this, all who were there
Opened wide their mouths and said: "So be it!"     330
Wretched Achior was summoned and did come,
Now quite happy, for the burden of his grief was
   lightened.
Judith said to him: "Today the God of Israel
Whom thou didst call our defense, know thou this,
He cut off the neck of the faithless one     335
By my hand, like a single hair;
So that thou seest whose, behold the head
Of him who in his arrogance did scorn God,
And who did say he would slay thee too
When he had smitten and enslaved this people."     340
Achior suddenly stirred when he caught sight[34]
Of the head which had driven him here threatening death;
And biding not a moment, he bowed his head in terror,
Like one at whom a lion suddenly doth roar.
When he raised his head, he knelt at Judith's feet,     345
Bowing deeply and saying: "Blessed art thou before God,
Thy God, Who through thee hath shown much mercy
   to us all;
His almighty power will everywhere be praised
Throughout the world, where'er thou shalt be known."

---

34. How Achior was frightened espying the head of Holofernes and did receive the Jewish faith and reside with his family in Bethulia till his death, seeing the power of the God of Israel.

## LIBRO ŠESTO

Obrativ se Judit, reče: »Slište, ča dim,
»Bog nam će posudit još milosti zatim;
»Zbodte kopjem jednim glavu tuj i pojte
»Gori na gradu s njim, ter umistiv ojte.
5   »Ništar se ne bojte; kada isteče dan,
»Odparvši vrat, projte s bukom, s oružjem van;
»Svaki prid gradom stan, da još nepoj doli,
»Ni se sa mista gan, ni kreni dotoli
»Dokol njih okoli, totu vas videće,
10   »'Zbuče se, ter poli šatora hodeće
»I šćiti kučeće budu budit njega,
»Ki se zbudit neće jur za vika svega.
»Ki kada vide ga prez glave ležeći,
»I karvava svega, hoće jih strah seći;
15   »Vi kad jih bižeći odzgoru vidite,
»Tad smini hiteći na njih oborite.
»Slobodno naprite, jer pod noge vaše
»Bog njimi poshite, dat jim će zle paše;
»Probavit će čaše kê su sinoć pili,
20   »Ginut će njih baše, vi ćete bit cili.
»I kojojno sili Mesopotamija
»Pridav se uhili i sva Cilicija,
»I još s njom Sirija, tuj ćete sada vi
»Rastirat, da svija nogami kud ne vî.«
25   Kako jim reče, svi tako učiniše.
Akior, jerbo vî kolika moć biše
Boga, kîm dobiše, poganski blud pusti,
U ki prî živiše, poča zakon bljusti;
Boga sarcem, usti jednoga počtova,

---

1. Kako Judit red dâ da zatiraju vojsku.
26. Akior se obrati.

## Book The Sixth

Turning to them Judith said:[1] "Hear what I say,
God will accord us yet more of His mercy for this.
Impale this head on the point of a spear and go
Up with it to the fortress, place it there and leave.
Fear nothing; when the day doth dawn,     5
Open the gates and go with noise and arms outside;
Let each man stand before the city, nor let him descend,
Nor may he move from the spot, nor set out,
Till all their camps, espying you,
Fall into confusion and race to the tent     10
With shields aclatter to awaken him
Who shall never again be awakened.
They who see him lying there without a head,
All bloody, will be seized with fear;
When ye see them running from that scene,     15
Go boldly forth and fall upon them.
Attack freely, for beneath your feet
God will cast them down, give them tare to eat;
They will drain the cups they have drunk this night,
Their leaders all shall perish, but ye will be whole.     20
And all that might to which Mesopotamia
And all Cilicia lamenting did submit,
And with them Syria, now shall ye
Disperse it, that it flee you headlong."
As she commanded, so did they all.     25
Achior, perceiving how great God's power was[2]
That conquered all, his pagan ways renounced
In which he formerly did live, and proclaimed the law;
With heart and lips he worshipped the one God,

---

1. How Judith giveth the order to pursue the troops.
2. Achior converteth.

30      Njega t' ne popusti; pokol se obrizova,
          Tuj vazda stanova sa obitil'ju svom,
          Sveto životova do konca u gradu tom.
      Vidiš li da u kom čoviku pravda jest,
          Još da ga triska grom, u dobro ga će unest;
35      Dobro će ustat i sest, vekše će nevolje
          Napokon ga navest na spasen'je bolje.
      Danica jur školje zrakom odivaše,
          Ter čarljeno polje suncu puščivaše;
          Sunce podivaše jur svitlu glavu van,
40      Jur svuda sivaše, jure bi bili dan:
      Zbodena na ostan na turnu tikva sta,
          I ništar ne postan, s oružjem družba sva
          Barom po vrata tâ buknu s bukom na dvor;
          Trumbitaš praskat jâ protiva vojsci zgor.
45      Po vojsci sta gromor, tekoše k šatoru,
          Ki bihu pod šator, staše prid komoru;
          Oružjem koporu, Oloferna zbučit
          Hteć, jer na zaporu ne smihu mu kučit.
      Zamani bi bučit, on se ne probudi:
50      Tim se jaše mučit. Shode' glave ljudi
          Vrataru, da zbudi njega sad, rekoše,
          Koga čuti sudi vojvode dojdoše
      Govore': »Zidoše od zakutak miši,
          »Ter nas zatekoše da boj biju piši.«
55      Tad Vagav ulišši, u dlan bi beritom.
          Za tim poposliši, mneć da spi s Juditom.
      Ne čuvši za svitom šušnja ni govora,
          Zadi parst za plitom, razmaknu zastora:
          Ugleda trup zgora gdi leži prez glave,
60      A pod njim je kora postilje karvave.
      Zavapi i plave razdri o se rube,
          I brade pahljave sidine oskube;
          Zatim sobom snube', plačan teče vidit
          Od skrovišća kruge u kê staše Judit.

---

37. Dan se učini.
61. Kako Vagav vratar zavapi ugledav Oloferna prez glave.

Who had not abandoned him; then he was circumcised,   30
And remained with them forever, with his household,
And did lead a holy life all his days in that city.
Dost thou see: if truth be in a man,
Even were he struck by lightning, he would reap good
　　from it;
He shall rise and sit well, ever greater perils   35
Shall all the more surely bring him to salvation.
The day star was clothing the crags with light,[3]
And the ruddy field made way for the sun;
The sun was already thrusting forth his luminous head,
Already it was brightening everywhere, already it was day:   40
Thrust on a spear point, a head rose from a tower;
And without further ado, arms ready, that company
Swarmed through the gates and burst into the clear;
The trumpeter began to trump to the troops from above.
A roar coursed through the troops, they hastened to
　　the tent;   45
Those before the tent stepped up to the sleeping chamber;
Clattering their arms, they sought to rouse Holofernes,
For they dared not knock on the bolted door.
In vain did they clatter, he did not awake:
This began to trouble them. The heads of the people   50
Went for the door keeper and ordered him to open
So that they might hear Holofernes' counsels,
And they said: "The mice have fled their holes,
And caught us by surprise to fight us now as soldiers."
Then Bagoas went in striking his cap 'gainst his palm,   55
Listening carefully, for he thought Holofernes slept
　　with Judith.
Hearing behind the veil neither rustling nor speech,
He poked his finger through the curtain and pulled
　　it back:
He looked down upon the corpse where it lay
　　without a head,
And the coverlets of the bed all in blood.   60
He did howl and rend his light blue garments,[4]
And pluck the scraggly grey hairs of his beard;
Then ran he all in tears to see himself
The treasure chambers wherein Judith lodged.

---

3. It becometh day.
4. How Bagoas the steward did howl espying Holofernes without his head.

65 Ne zastav ju, hitit jâ da van isteče;
   Istekši jâ vapit: »Jedna žena«, reče,
   »Židovinka, spletče prugo u sem dvoru,
   »Priročno poleče Nabuk'donosoru.
   »Evo u svû komoru Oloferne kopni
70 »Na postilji goru, na njemu glave ni!«
   Asirski baše tî glas kada slišiše,
   Obojmeknuše svi i svite razdriše.
   Svi se pristrašiše, kako komu gavun
   Vali zbiv odniše argutlu i tamun;
75 Dimajući garbun jidrom paha, hahće,
   Miša s morem salbun, on od straha darhće:
   Takim strahom dahće bijeno sarce ovih,
   Plač ter vapaj bahće, i jur obide svih;
   Ne osta karv u njih, i vidiv na grad dil
80 Udov Olofernjih, strah jih je veći bil.
   Marmor je svuda vril, smete se vas okol;
   Starknja usta od sil, svak je bižat obol.
   Kako kada sokol u nebo se vija,
   Jato se ptic odzdol široko razvija,
85 Ča pri môre svija, naprid se pojima,
   Jer ga strah zabija, duše ne pojima:
   Tako tada njima bojazan micaše,
   Simo-tamo svima po polju starkaše.
   Svaki se bojaše, jer Betulijani
90 Oružnih hust staše nad njimi u strani;
   Ki vidiv da bani asirski odbigoše,
   S onih gornjih stani vičući stekoše.
   Stižući bodoše mnozih šćipačami,
   Mnozih posikoše po pleću sabljami;
95 Mnozi ki lugami na konjih bižahu,
   Sabijeni praćami legoše u prahu.
   Nevidom svijahu; nigdar toke sile
   U toliku strahu, ja mnju, nisu bile,
   Kud su god hodile, ni kih moći manje

---
73. Prilika.
78. Kako se vojska pristraši i poča bižati.
84. Prilika.

He did not find her there, and hastened to go out;　　　65
Outside he began to cry: "One woman," said he,
"Of the Hebrews, having set up her loom in this court,
Hath shamefully ensared King Nabuchodonosor.
Behold, in his chamber, doth Holofernes rot,
There, upon his bed, lieth he without a head!"　　　70
When the Assyrian leaders heard these words,
To a man they did wail and rend all their garments.
All were afeared, like the man from whom the waves,[5]
His cabin destroyed, carried off rod and rudder;
The sou'wester whistleth and filleth his sail,　　　75
Mixeth the sea and the sands, while he trembleth in terror:
From like terror do they gasp, hearts pounding in
　　their chests,
Weeping and wailing grab hold and overwhelm them;[6]
No blood remained in them, and when on the walls
　　of the city
They saw a member of Holofernes' body, their
　　fear grew greater.　　　80
A clamour rose roundabout, the whole camp was
　　in confusion;
Thus began the rout of the army, each fled his own way.
As when the hawk riseth in the heavens,
And a flock of birds flieth up from below,[7]
Gathering together as fast as possible, to move forward,　　　85
For fear presseth them on, nor can they catch their breath:
So did fear drive them at that time,
Hither and thither it scattered them 'cross the land.
Each was afraid, for a multitude of well-armed
Bethulians stood o'er them all on the heights;　　　90
Seeing that the leaders of the Assyrians were in flight,
Those did race down shouting from their hilltops.
When they caught them, pierced they them with
　　their spears,
And hacked them with their swords through their
　　shoulderblades;
Many who fled on horseback through the woods,　　　95
Were struck down by slings, and they lay in the dust.
They disappeared from sight; never hath such a great force
Been in such fear, I believe, where e'er they turned,
Nor hath a smaller army e'er attacked them

---
5. A comparison.
6. How the troops were frightened and began to flee.
7. A comparison.

100     Jesu naskočile, ni tirale hlanje.
        Ozija, da na nje od gradov pripuste,
            Jer će biti sa nje, da jih ne upuste;
            I da ljudi huste zaskoče na cistih,
            Mače, ki to zuste tičući po mistih:
105     To pisa u listih, kê kada pročtaše,
            Od mist onih istih harlo se sticaše,
            Ter ti jih tiraše, derući bijući,
            Gdi su njih mejaše deri dopirući.
        Meju tim slazući od Betulije, kî
110         Grada čuvajući ostali bihu svi,
            Asirski okol gdi biše ostao pust,
            Mnogu pratež ondi razuzeše u hust.
        Kako vinograd gust, kad je voće zrilo,
            Koga ne bude bljust pudar ni pudilo,
115         Jato ga pokrilo čvarljak, grozd ne ojde,
            Kad se je najilo, s punom gvacom pojde:
        Tako svaki dojde šiju nakarcavši,
            I u gradu projde, okol rasakavši;
            Za njimi prignavši, ča gonit mogoše,
120         Ki, vojsku zagnavši, s dobitjem pridoše.
        Tuj blago snesoše od asirske sile,
            I ča dotekoše, svim riše da dile;
            Nikogar ne uhile, svi biše bogati,
            I po pune zdile jaše blagovati.
125     Jaše napijati, Bogu hvale daje',
            I veseli stati redom počitaje',
            Gdi ki dostizaje' biše koga ubil,
            Gdi ki priticaje' biše put zaskočil.
        Bože, kolikih sil kolika gardina,
130         Kolikih slava dil i hvale visina,
            Koli vred izlinja prebiv se na polil
            Tako Bog načinja svih ki su oholi.
        Svi gradi okoli činiše vesel'ja

---

101. Ozija mače i liste pisa po mistih da tiraju vojsku kâ bižaše.
113. Prilika.
129. Protiv oholim.

Or more easily set them to rout. 100
Ozias did command an attack from the cities,[8]
For they would be equal to them, and should not
   let them pass,
And that a multitude of the host should go out
   to the highways,
Drawing their swords to proclaim this in all places.
When they read the scrolls in which this was written, 105
They hastened together from all these places,
And did pursue them, thrashing and beating
And pressing them on to the borders of their lands.
At the same time they did descend from Bethulia
Who had remained behind to protect it, 110
To the Assyrian camp which now stood empty,
And they took great heaps of booty.
Like as the dense vineyard, when the fruit is ripe,[9]
If it not be guarded by the vine dresser and a scarecrow,
A flock of starlings will cover it, no grape can escape, 115
And having eaten their fill, they fly off with full wattle:
So each returned bent down beneath the load
And entered the city, having plundered the camp;
Behind them brought they in what they could
Who as victors returned from dispersing the foe. 120
Here they assembled all the goods of the Assyrians,
And they who came late were also told to take a share;
Nor was any aggrieved, all did become rich,
And began to dine from bowls brimming o'er,
And to drink their fill, giving thanks to God, 125
And to rejoice, as they told in turn
Who had killed whom, and where and by what means,
And who in hot pursuit had cut off whose escape.
O Lord! How great the pride of such great armies,[10]
The glory of such deeds, how high the heights
   of boasting, 130
How quickly it all passeth when their strength
   is shattered!
Thus doth God treat all them who are haughty.
All the cities 'round about made merry

---

8. Ozias sent swords and letters to the cities that they pursue the troops which were fleeing.
9. A comparison.
10. Against the arrogant.

*I na svetom stoli klaše mnoga tel'ja;*
135 *Cvitja tere zel'ja tla su natrusili,*
*Borja tere jel'ja zide su nadili;*
*Trublje su trubili, bubnji su bubnjali,*
*Svirale svirili, cindre privartali;*
*Hvalu Bogu dali u pisnih pojući,*
140 *Tance su igrali, svitila žegući;*
*Hvalu još dajući dilu Juditinu,*
*Kim dobivajući skupiše litinu;*
*I gradi u istinu zdrišiše straha grop,*
*Ki mnjahu da zginu pod toke sile snop.*
145 *Eliakim, veli pop od Jerosolime,*
*Noseć smočen isop kropljaše da snime*
*Nečistoć onime ki se ockvarniše*
*Svite martvih prime', kih zagnav ubiše.*
*Za njim ti grediše popovi mnogi zbor,*
150 *S njim grede' dopriše Betuliji na dvor;*
*I kad pram njim odzgor Judita iskasi,*
*Svakoga ju govor s hvalom dobročasi.*
*Riše joj: »Slava si Jerosolime sve,*
*»Sva radost naša si, počten'je zemlje sê;*
155 *»Jere je sarce tvê muški se nosilo,*
*»Tobom je strane ove misto oživilo.*
*»A sve je to bilo, jer čistoću tvoju*
*»Pogleda Bog milo i dâ t' milost svoju;*
*»Jer sta u pokoju, muža ne poznavši,*
160 *»I u svetih broju, parvi ti umarvši.*
*»Bog tebe zazvavši sparti nas brimena,*
*»I tebe obravši proslavi t' imena:*
*»Tim blagoslovljena biti ćeš po sve dni,*
*»Biti ćeš blažena gdi dobru konca ni!«*
165 *Takovom nju oni besidom slavljahu*

---

145. Kako od Jerosolime dojdoše popove i hvališe Juditu.
148. Jer u zakonu ockvarnjen biše ki se takniše martva človika; pop jih očišćaše škropeći vodom u kôj biše lug krave ćarljene, močeći u njoj isop.
157. Vij dostojanstvo čistinje udovičke.

And slaughtered many a calf upon the altars;
Did strew the ground with flowers and greens, 135
Decked the walls with pine branches and fir trees;
They trumped upon trumpets, drummed upon drums,
Piped the pipes and struck the cymbals;
They praised God aloud in hymns of praise,
Danced their dances as they lit candelabra; 140
Praise gave they as well to Judith's deed,
By which they were able to bring in the harvest.
And the cities undid in truth that knot of fear,
Which once were sure to perish 'fore the conquerer's might.
Joakim, the great high priest of Jerusalem,[11] 145
Bearing moistened hyssop, splashed it on them,
To lift the taint from those who were unclean
From touching the garments of them whom they had driven to death.[12]
After him came a great assembly of the elders,
And with him they arrived before Bethulia. 150
And Judith hastened down to stand before them,
Each one did hail her with his words of praise.
They said to her: "Thou art the glory of all Jerusalem,
Thou art our joy, the honour of this land;
Thine heart hath borne itself in manly fashion, 155
Through thee this place hath livened other realms.
And all because God hath regarded thy purity[13]
In His mercy, and given thee His grace;
For thou hast remained at peace, in the company of saints,
Not knowing an husband, for thine died before thee. 160
In summoning thee God cast off our burdens,
And in choosing thee hath glorified thy name:
Thus shalt thou be blessed all thy days long,
And blissful in the place where good ne'er endeth."
In just such words did they praise her, 165

---

11. How the elders came from Jerusalem and did praise Judith.
12. For in the law he is defiled who toucheth the garments of a dead man; the priest did purify them, sprinkling them with water in which was the ash of a red heifer and hyssop dipped therein.
13. Viz., the dignity of widowly purity.

        *I Bogu pokloni s njom prikazivahu;*  
        *Ki godi imahu Olofernja blaga,*  
        *K njoj ga prinošahu, ona Bogu dâ ga.*  
    *A sad veras snaga mojih nju hvaliti*  
170    *Slaba jest i naga; ništar manj' naviti*  
    *Neću se šćediti hvale, koko mogu,*  
    *Jer se iščuditi dilu nje ne mogu.*  
    *Sminost svoju mnogu ukaza Delbora,*  
        *Kad razbi nalogu vojske kon Tabora,*  
175    *Da čast togaj stvora s Barakom razdili*  
        *I s ljudmi njih dvora ki biše u tom dili.*  
    *Jahele još sili hvala se pomina,*  
        *Jer kralja uhili od Kane Jabina,*  
    *Kadano bi smina Sisaru ubiti,*  
180    *Kîno k njemu plina općaše nositi;*  
*Da to učiniti sama a samomu,*  
    *I čaval zabiti jur pristrašenomu*  
    *Laglje je ner tomu ki steć mev svojimi*  
    *Prićaše svakomu da će vladat svimi.*  
185  *Još je dika s timi i onoj kâ Sibi*  
    *Svîtom svojim snimi glavu kako ribi:*  
    *Grad jur na pogibi tad Abela biše,*  
    *I u toj potribi tim se slobodiše;*  
    *Da toj učiniše jednomu vele jih,*  
190  *A njoj hvala biše kâ na to svede jih;*  
    *Da kâ mev veće jih sama vojvodu ubi,*  
    *I tim zatira svih, koli slavnija bi?*

---

    169. Hvala smin'ja i hrabrosti Juditine.

    173. Delbora proročica i Barak sašad s gore Tabor s deset tisuć sinov izraelskih, razbiše veliku silu vojske kralja Jabina od Kananeje prid kimi biše Sisara.

    177. Sisara: ovi sâm bižeći, pribiže k Jaheli, kâ budući od puka izraelskoga, čineći se da ga će skriti, pokri ga pak mu zabi čaval jedan u slipo oko i ubi ga.

    185. Siba smetnju učini protiv Davidu, hteći gospodovati. Vojvode Davidovi opsedoše ga u Abelu. Žena razumna, da se grad ne razaspe, čini mu glavu usići, varže ju njim niz mir; zato se vojska dviže, a grad osta prost.

And make their offerings with her before God;
Whosoever had the wealth of Holofernes
Brought it unto her, and she gave it to God.
And now the power of these my verses to praise her[14]
Is poor and threadbare; nonetheless I shall not stint        170
To weave her praises with all my might,
For I cannot but admire her deeds to their full measure.
Deborah her boldness showed in great abundance[15]
When she dispersed the armed multitudes at Tabor,
But a portion of that deed she shared with Barak,           175
And with the people of that land who did take part.
Praise is also given to Jael's might[16]
For she brought Jabin down, the king of Canaan,
When she waxed bold to slay Sisera
Whose wont it was to bring captives to the king;            180
But this she did when he was by himself
And hammered in the nail when he was stiff with fear:
'Twere easier far than slaying one amidst his troops,
One who threatened to conquer the entire world.
Her glory might as well be compared to hers[17]             185
Who did advise they cut off Sheba's head like a fish's:
The city of Abel of Beth-maachah was on the brink
    of falling
But she did free it in its hour of need.
Because they were many who did it to one,
Glory belongeth to her who brought them all to it.          190
But she who in their midst did slay their own leader,
And thus destroy them all, is she not more glorious still?

---

14. Laud to Judith's boldness and bravery.
15. Deborah the prophetess and Barak, having come down from Mount Tabor with ten thousand of the sons of Israel, dispersed the great force of Jabin's army, king of Canaan, which were commanded by Sisera.
16. Sisera: fleeing himself, he ran to Jael, who, being of the people of Israel, did pretend that she would conceal him; having covered him over she drove a nail into his forehead and slew him.
17. Sheba made a revolt against David, for he wanted to rule. David's captains besieged him in Abel. A wise woman, that the city not be destroyed, had his head cut off, and threw it down to them at the foot of the city wall; the army did then lift the siege, and the city was freed.

        Palas smila ne bi toko ni Diana,
        Prizvavši još k sebi s strilami Peana;
195     Ni kâno Trojana kralju nos odrubi,
        Sasvim dešperana, jer joj sina zgubi.
        I kêno suzubi muških vojask stahu,
        Jake kako dubi, hrabro se nošahu,
        Na konjih ticahu prez sasa desnoga,
200     Gdino prižimahu kopja bodežnoga:
        Ne bi smile toga u obraz pozriti,
        A smila je koga Judita zgubiti.
        Kôj poni Hipoliti, kôj Pantasileji,
        More se saviti kruna, kâ je oveji?
205     Nî slave takeji dostojna, kâ kada
        Ču na svojoj meji Babilona grada,
        Da se sam oblada, od nje se odvargši,
        Opet ga podklada, kose ne uzvargši.
        Ni kêno ner svargši neprijatelja s konj
210     I život mu stargši, mečem sikuć po nj,
        — Takov tada zakon biše mev Zamate —
        Nimahu taj poklon da budu mužate.

---

193. Palas piše se oružna, jer dijahu da je božica od arvanje; Diana dijahu da je božica od lova, zato se piše sa strilami. Pean ali Apolo, nje brat, tokoj nosi strile.

195. Ovo je bila Hekuba, žena kralja od Troje Prijama, kâ čineći se nič otajno govorit Polinestoru, kralju od Tracije, nos mu odgrize; jer on biše zgubio sina nje Polidora koga k njemu biše poslao Prijam s blagom mnozim bojeći se. Kad Garci podsedoše Troju i kad zgibe Troja, on ubi Polidora za uzeti sebi blago kô biše donio.

197. Suzub muških vojask stahu Amazone, kê da mogu bolje kopjem vladati, prisicahu sas desni.

203. Hipolita i Pantasileja jesu bile poglavice od Amazoni.

205. Ovo je bila Semiramis, kraljica od Asirije, kâ kose pletući ču da se je Babilon od nje odvargao: ne splete druge kose dokla ga opet ne prija.

211. Zamate bihu ki stahu na usta Tanaje rike, s kimi i žene vojevahu kê ne mogahu pojat muža, dokle ne ubijahu neprijatelja svojom rukom. Taj zakon biše.

Neither Pallas nor Diana[18] were ever so brave,
Who did summon to themselves Pean and his arrows,
Nor that Trojan woman who tore off the king's nose[19]  195
In her grief, for that he had slain her son.
And those women who faced the ranks of men,[20]
Powerful as oaktrees, they carried themselves bravely,
They raced their horses though they'd lost their
  right breast
So that they might grasp their sharp spears
  the more firmly:  200
They would not have dared to look upon the face
Whom Judith did dare to slay.
For which Hippolyta, which Pentheselea then[21]
Might one plait the crown that is on this one's head?
Nor is she worthy of such glory who upon hearing[22]  205
That Babylon, a city of her own realm,
Had overthrown her rule and sought to rule itself,
Combed not her hair till she had retaken it.
Nor are they who cast the enemy from their horses
And shortened their life with a stroke of the sword–  210
Such was the custom then among the Sarmatians[23]–
For they could not wed till they had accomplished this.

---

18. Pallas is depicted with armaments, for she was called the goddess of battle; Diana was called the goddess of the hunt, therefore she was depicted with arrows. Phoebus or Apollo, her brother, also bore arrows.
19. This was Hecuba, the wife of King Priam of Troy, who, pretending she had something to say in secret to Polymestor, the King of Thrace, did bite off his nose; for he had slain her son Polidorus whom Priam had sent to him out of fear, with many goods. When the Greeks besieged Troy and Troy perished, he killed Polidorus in order to take the goods that he had brought.
20. Opposed to the troops of men stood the Amazons, who, so that they might better wield the spear, did cut off their right nipple.
21. Hippolyta and Pentheselea were leaders of the Amazons.
22. This was Semiramis, the Queen of Assyria, who, whilst plaiting her hair, did hear that Babylon had revolted against her: she did not plait the other braid until she had retaken it.
23. The Sarmatians were they who stood at the mouth of the River Tanais; with them their women also did battle, for they could not take a husband until they had slain an enemy with their own hand. This was their law.

              *Ni kê Pira s bate rekoše odrinut*
              *Ispod Sparte da te, ali s njom izginut;*
215           *Zato od nje minut inamo ne htiše,*
              *Pir osta ostinut, jer se i one riše.*
              *Ni kê, kad razbiše Cimbre rimske sile,*
              *Same se ubiše, jer nisu hotile*
              *Da budu sidile žive pod inimi,*
220           *Ner u boj hodile tada bihu s kimi.*
              *Ni ona kâ primi od Meleagra čast,*
              *Jer parva mev svimi prostrili prascu mast,*
              *Prascu ki svaku slast kalidonskih dubrav*
              *— Toku imaše vlast — gubljaše ne sustav.*
225           *Svih tih zajedno stav, ter Judite hvale*
              *S hvalami njih pristav, reć ćeš: njih su male,*
              *Pri toj su ostale kako pri hartu zec,*
              *Pri sokolku gale, pri sunaccu misec.*
              *Njih jošće slave brec po zemlji boboni,*
230           *Po zemlji njih je tec — a na nebi je nî;*
              *Juditina zvoni i visoko gori,*
              *Gdi ju s sobom poni, gdi su an'jelski kori,*
              *Gdi su rajski dvori, Kerubin, Serafin,*
              *Gdi su svetih zbori, gdi Bog i božji sin,*
235           *Gdi je svitlost prez tmin, radost prez pečali,*
              *Gdi nî konac ni fin dobru nje ni hvali.*
              *A sad, ki ste iskali segaj svita slavu,*
              *Ki ste nastojali imit slug zastavu,*
              *Ki li dvigši glavu vojske ste vodili*

---

213. Spartani ali Lacedemonezi, videći da jih će podsesti kralj Pir, hotihu žene dati van na otocih; one ne htiše, hoteći i one braniti grad ali s njim zajedno poginuti; i tako se nosiše, da jih on ne more prijati.

217. Cimbri sada se zovu Flamengi. Naskočiše Italiju, učiniše škodu veliku Rimnjanom. Marij razbi jih. Žene, kê s njimi bihu, ubiše se da ne pridu žive u ruke neprijatelj svojih.

221. Ovo je bila Atlanta, hći Ceneja kralja od Arkadije, kâ s Meleagrom i s inimi gospodičići garčkimi naskočivši prasca divjega u Kalidoniju, parva ga ustrili; i kad ga ubiše, Meleagar ga njoj prisudi.

237. Protiv tašćoj slavi.

Nor are those women who claimed they would drive off
   Pyrrhus[24]
With clubs from Sparta, or perish with the city:
For that they desired never to part from it,                       215
Pyrrhus did perish, because they too did fight.
Nor are they who, as the Roman legions crushed
   the Cimbri,[25]
Did kill themselves, for they desired not
To continue life 'neath the rule of others,
But went out with the men to fight in the fray.            220
Nor she who did accept the honour from Meleager[26]
For that she first of all did pierce the hog's fat,
The hog who did all the joy of the Calydonian wood–
Such was his power!–ceasely destroy.
Put all those together, and then compare                    225
Them with Judith's glory, their glories would pale,
They lag behind her as the hare behind the whippet,
The gull behind the falconet, the moon behind the sun.
Their fame doth resound throughout all the earth,
Earthly their achievements–but heaven knoweth them not:   230
Judith's fame ringeth to the loftiest height,
Whither she doth bear them herself, where angelic choirs,
Where gardens of paradise, Cherubim, Seraphim dwell,
Where the saints gather together, where live God
   and His Son,
Where there is light without shadow, joy without pain,    235
Where her praise and her virtue never know an end.
And now ye who have lusted for the glory of this world,[27]
Who have desired hordes of slaves to do your bidding,
Who have raised your heads and led out armies

---

24. The Spartans or Lacedemonians, seeing that King Pyrrhus would besiege them, resolved to place their women outside the city on islands; they did not wish to go, desiring also to protect the city or perish together with it; and they so bore themselves that he could not take it.
25. The Cimbri are now called the Flemings. They attacked Italy, causing the Romans much damage. Marius shattered them. The women who were with them slew themselves lest they be taken live by their enemies.
26. This was Atalanta, the daughter of King Ceneus of Arcadia, who, whilst hunting with Meleager and other Greek princelings for the wild boar in Calydonia, shot it first; and when they had killed it, Meleager ajudged it to be hers.
27. Against vainglory.

240      *I svita daržavu poda se podbili;*
*Ki ni svojoj sili, ni svomu blagu broj*
*Reći ste umili, živeći u pokoj*
*I u raskoši svoj: vijte je l' dika ta*
*Vaša takmena ovoj ka se Juditi dâ?*
245      *Ona se sada sja, vi ste u tamnosti;*
*Nju radost obuja, vi ste plačni dosti;*
*Ona je u milosti kralja nebeskoga,*
*Vi ste u gardosti djavla paklenoga.*
*Tim ti se svakoga slava vred zamini,*
250      *Ki zabivši Boga, svit ljubi i cini;*
*Da tako ne čini presveta Judita,*
*Zato Bog učini da je blagovita;*
*Da se po sva lita i po vikov vike*
*Hvala nje počita, nje pronose dike*
255      *Po mora, po rike, po zemlje okol vas,*
*I gdi sve vernike sabire vičnji spas.*
*Jur poni svaki nas nju htijmo sliditi,*
*Jur počnimo danas pobožno živiti:*
*Moliti, postiti, ponizit dušu i pût,*
260      *Oštrine nositi, gizdav odvrići skut;*
*Daržat čistinje put, telu ne dati last,*
*Da svagdan truda prut, da nam ne dâ napast;*
*U svem Bogu dat čast, a ne moći svojoj:*
*Da Duha Sveta mast pomaga vazda njoj.*
265      *Utišen'ja pokoj diliti ubozim,*
*Prostiti nepokoj uražen'ja mnozim,*
*I svakim nemozim pomoći ne kratit,*
*I kâ svakim mozim s ljubicom se obratit;*
*Ljubav ljubvom platit, ljubvom i gardinu,*
270      *Za zlih Bogu vapit da jim dâ dobrinu,*
*Ljubiti istinu, laže se čuvati,*
*Ufan'ja slatčinu nigdar ne puščati:*
*To t' su bili pati, za kê Bog gospodin*
*Dostoja se obrati Juditu, kako t' dim,*
275      *Po njoj da zgasi dim Oloferna ljuta*
*I slobod poda svim ki čekahu pruta.*
*I ki jur ni muta nimahu ča piti,*

To trample the wide earth beneath your feet; 240
Ye who were unable to count the number
Of your arms or your goods, as ye lived in peace
And great comfort, regard ye this: can that fame of yours
Compete with that which is Judith's by right?
Now she doth shine, while ye sit in the dark, 245
Joy encompasseth her, ye are more than mournful;
She is in the grace of the Lord of the Heavens,
Ye bespeak the wickedness of the Lord of Hell.
Into that doth the glory turn of each one
Who, forgetting God, loveth and cherisheth this world; 250
But thus the most saintly Judith doth not do,
For which reason God hath ordained for her great
    rewards;
That through all years, throughout all generations,
Her praises be recited, her glories be told
On the sea, all rivers, o'er the whole earthly orb, 255
Where'er eternal salvation gathereth in the faithful.
Let each one of us, then, follow her example,
Let us each, from today, live a pious life:
Pray, fast, humble soul and fleshly parts,
Wear hair-shirts, cast off immodest dress; 260
Keep pure the body, give the flesh no respite,
But daily make it labour, lest it lead us to the pit;
In all honour God and not our own power:
That the balm of the Holy Ghost might ever help us.
The solace of peace share with the poor, 265
The distress of anger forgive the many
And cease not to aid the weak in their need,
With the powerful conduct yourselves in love;
Recompense love with love, with love repay evil,
For the wicked pray ye to God that He grant them
    goodness; 270
Love the truth, keep yourselves clear of lies,
And the joy of believing never neglect:
'Twas for these reasons that the Lord our God
Did deign ennoble Judith, as I have said,
That by her He did extinguish wild Holofernes' vainglory 275
And give freedom to them who expected the whip.
And those who had left not e'en the dregs to drink,

Lica suha, žuta pričali nositi:
Po njoj jih nasiti obil'ja mnogoga,
280    Po njoj jih naparti blaga još svakoga.
Svi puci cić toga veselit se jaše,
Ova hvaleć Boga radosno pojaše;
Svak, ki totu staše, uši gori napan,
Pisan nje slišaše, riči svoje zapan.
285    Ovo biše pisan kû jâ govoriti:
»Otvorite usan, počnite hvaliti
»Boga i slaviti, u cimbale zvone',
»Kitare udriti, psalam peti tone:
»Bog bo potar one ki rat podvigoše,
290    »Onim milost klone ki stav uzdahoše;
»Zgubit nas dojdoše asirski odbori,
»Toga ne stigoše, Bog njimi obori.
»Dolce, varhe, gori bihu pokrilili,
»Vod naših izvori bihu zavalili;
295    »Požgat su pritili sela naša i stane,
»Žene s dicom htili vest u svoje strane,
»Inim dati rane, svih smartno sikući;
»Da Bog naš nas brane', njih slomi tukući,
»Karvavca dajući pod oblastju žene,
300    »Sile njih hotući da budu smetene.
»Zatoj ti spletene biše mnogim strahom,
»Zazbične i bijene karv smišaše s prahom,
»Kê s nesmirnim bahom bihu nastupile,
»A pak s ovim gradom bit se nisu smile.
305    »Oloferna bile nisu mnozih ruke,
»Ni ga naskočile vojske, napan luke,
»Ni pojamši suke žiganti nesmirni,
»Ni od meči zuke ljudi boju birni;
»Da u suknji pirni Judit, hći Merara,
310    »I pameti virni pozorom ga vara,
»Svarže s sebe stara udovna odila,
»I sta na njoj zgara zlato, biser, svila.
»Rumena ter bila lica svâ učini,
»Pojde kako vila: tim njega prihini,

---

285. Kantika ali pisan Juditina.

So that their faces began to turn sallow,
By her did He satisfy them with rich abundance,
By her did He fill them with all good things. 280
All the peoples as a result began to rejoice.
She, praising God, joyously did sing;
Those standing nearby did prick up their ears,
And listen to her hymn, drawing the words into
their hearts.
This was the song that she began to recite:[28] 285

"Open your lips, begin to praise
And glorify God sounding on the cymbals,
Strike the timbrels, tune unto Him psalms:
For God hath broken them that made war,
Shown mercy to them that sighed in prayer; 290
The hordes of Assur had come to slay us,
They achieved that not, for God o'erturned them.
Vales and hills and mountains they did cover,
They trampled the springs of our fresh water;
They threatened to burn our settlements and homes, 295
To lead off our women and children to their lands,
To inflict mighty wounds and hack others to death;
But our God did protect us, beat them and break them,
Did give the bloodthirsty into the power of a woman,
So that He might confuse the forces of the enemy. 300
And they were compassed about by great fear,
Broken and beaten, they mixed their blood with dust,
They in great swagger had fallen upon us,
They did not dare to wage war with this city.
Holofernes was not struck by the hands of many men, 305
Nor was he overtaken by armies with stretched bows,
Nor by huge giants wielding their bludgeons,
Nor by warriors used to the clang of iron blades;
Rather, in festive garb, Judith, Merar's daughter,
Mindful of her faith in God, seduced him with her gaze, 310
She cast off the garments of her widowhood
And put on gold, pearls and clothes of silk.
She made herself rouged and, whitening her cheeks,
She set off like a sprite: thus she took the man in,

---

28. The canticle or song of Judith.

315  »Tim sarce u pini stavi mu pak glavu
   »Odkla kako svinji ali kako bravu.
   »Ćut bi kako lavu vijan'je plača njih,
   »Bižeći po travu kad vidiše mojih;
   »Ki jih tukoše svih, goneći kako skot,
320  »Sto tisuć biše kih i četarsta krat stot.
   »Božja bo to bi hot, tako da bigaše
   »Okola pustiv plot: naši jih stizaše,
   »Naši jih deraše, oni predajući,
   »Naši jih rizaše, oni se ne rvući.
325  »Zato sad pojući recmo u radosti:
   »Bože svemogući, kolike s' kriposti!
   »Ki tvojoj jakosti mogu bit opori?
   »Sve od tvê strahosti trepi, jer sve stvori.
   »Ganut se je gori i svita zemlji svoj,
330  »Kada ti odzgori sardit pogledaš k njoj;
   »Da strah u kih je tvoj, bojeć se zgrišiti,
   »Ti jim ćeš dat pokoj, ti jih uzvišiti.
   »A kino prititi narodu budu mom,
   »Ti jih ćeš suditi i starti rukom tvom;
335  »Pasti će s moćju svom u oganj neugasljit,
   »Bit pića čarvu tom ki nigdare ni sit.« —
   Zatim puk jâ hitit u Jerosolim pojt,
   Bogu se poklonit ki jih li ne hti ojt;
   Hteć barzo tamo dojt, putem se varviše,
340  Prišad, u tempal projt po vrata nagliše.
   Saužge činiše gori na oltare,
   Zavite svaršiše prikazavši dare;
   Stahu redom žare gdi se umivahu,
   I tamjana pare svuda se vijahu.
345  Mirisi vonjahu, zvonjahu psaltiri,
   Popovi pojahu, odpivahu miri;
   Sjahu kandeliri zlati, sedmostruci,
   I bili dupliri, kako puri luci.
   Dvigši obi ruci, a prignuv kolina
350  Klanjahu se puci hvaleć Gospodina;

---

341. Saužgi djački se zovu holocausta.

Thus she set his heart in torment, cut off his head, 315
Like that of a swine or a yearling sheep.
Their cry was like unto that of a lion's roar
When, espying my troops, they raced 'cross the fields;
And they did slay them all, leading them like cattle,
Them who had numbered one hundred forty thousand. 320
For such was God's will that they should flee,
Abandoning the safety of their camp; our men did catch them,
Ours did smite them, they surrendered,
Ours did cleave them, they did not resist.
So let us raise now a joyful song: 325
Lord God Almighty! How great is Thy strength!
Who can withstand Thy power?
All trembleth in fear before Thee, Creator of all things.
Mountains and all the earth must move before Thee
When Thou from above dost cast down Thine
   angry glance: 330
But to them who fear Thee and are mindful of their sins,
Thou shalt give peace and raise them up.
But them who breathe threats against my people
Thou wilt judge and wipe away with Thine hand;
By Thy power will they fall into unquenchable fire, 335
Be food for the worm whose hunger endeth never."

Then did the people hasten to go to Jerusalem
To bow before God Who would not abandon them;
They swarmed o'er the road in their haste to arrive,
Once in the temple, they rushed at the doors. 340
They burned offerings and sacrifices[29] on the altars,
Fulfilled their vows and made their gifts;
Nearby stood urns wherein they did wash,
And the vapours of incense wafted on high.
The odours did spread, the psalteries sounded, 345
The priests chanted and the walls echoed back;
Seven-branched candelabra of gold stood there,
And white waxen candles that seemed made of light.
Raising both their hands and bending their knees,
The people knelt before the Lord and did praise him; 350

---

29. "Offerings and sacrifices" are called "holocausta" in the clerical [djački] language. (Marulić explains the Croatian word "saužgi," burnt offerings with a Latin word–HC.)

Vesela družina mnogu čini radost,
Jer kîm biše tmina, slaja jim bi svitlost.
Juditina milost oružje pridava,
Olofernja oholost kim se oružava,
355 Koga joj tad dava puk nje kad u gradu
S plinom ujahava, vesel glade' bradu.
U tempal da dadu tuj, reče, čast Bogu,
I k tomu nadadu karzno na kom nogu
Steriše, ki mnogu oholast odside
360 Kad ona nebogu glavu mu odkide.
Tri miseci side' u Jerosolimi,
Tuj pijući i jide', Judita sa svimi
Vele veselimi blagdane radosti
Čini, jere primi dobitja milosti.
365 Paka u naglosti svi se razidoše,
Kîno bihu gosti, svak k svojim idoše;
Da parvo pojdoše Juditu združiti,
Od nje odidoše čtovani i siti.
Ona posta biti slovuća po svitu,
370 Počaše ju čtiti više svih uznitu;
Zatim vazda svitu udovne čistinje
Nosi na se zditu, odkol umri muž nje.
Do stare starinje živi u počten'ju;
Lakesis trudi nje ču tad u preden'ju,
375 Kloto u varćen'ju, Atropos pririza,
Kad ona življen'ju sto i pet lit stiza.
Grob ju on poviza u ki joj muž biše,
Veće se ne dviza od tud gdi ju skriše;
Duh se veseliše da — puti tamnice

---

374. Ovoj su tri kê predu naš život. Lakesis tumači se ždribnica, jer ždribe miče života našega potežući žicu s preslice. Kloto vartnica, jer varti vretenom sučući tuj žicu. Atropos tumači se: prez obraćenja, jer se obratiti ne more mitom ni jednim da ne čini konac života našega žicu tu pririzujući. Ovej tri biližaju tri vrimena života našega: vrime kô će biti, kô jest, kô je bilo. Kô će biti, isteže žicu; kô jest, varti ju ali suče; kô je bilo, jur smotanu žicu pririzuje svemu čineći konac. Ovdi zato di da trudne jur bihu Juditin život predući, jer ona dugo živi: sto i pet lit.

The happy multitude waxed most joyous,
For who was in darkness findeth light all the sweeter.
Judith graciously did offer all the stuff
With which once Holofernes had equipped himself,
The stuff which the people, returning to the city           355
With their booty, had given her, stroking their beards
  in satisfaction.
She instructed them thus to honour God in His temple,
Also to give the pelts on which the feet
Were placed of him who left off his arrogant ways
When Judith did sever from him his wretched head.          360

Three months did she tarry in Jerusalem,
Drinking and eating; Judith did with all
Make the holidays of joy a most happy occasion,
For she had partaken of the grace of conquest.
Then all went their own way in haste                        365
Who had been visiting, each to his own inheritance;
But first they went to take leave of Judith,
They left her presence honoured and sated.
She became famous throughout the world,
And they began to honour her above all others;             370
From the time her husband had died she began
Always to wear the garb of widow's chastity.
Till ripe old age she lived in honour;
Lachesis felt pain in her measuring,[30]
Clotho in her spinning, Atropos in snipping,               375
When Judith reached the hundred-fifth year of her life.
That grave was made ready where her husband had
  been laid,
Never again riseth she from the place where they hid her;
Her soul rejoiced for that she, made free

---

30. These are the three who weave our lives. Lachesis is interpreted as caster of lots, for she casteth the lots of our lives in drawing the thread off the spindle. Clotho is the spinner, for she twisting the thread spinneth it upon the wheel. Atropos is interpreted: without returning, for she cannot be induced to turn back, lest she end our lives in cutting the thread. The three of these bring together the three seasons of our lives: the season which shall be, which is, which was. Which shall be: she draweth out the thread. Which is: she spinneth or twisteth it. Which was: she cutteth the wound thread, making an end to all. Thus here it is said that they were fatigued in spinning Judith's life for she lived so long: one hundred and five years.

380 Izbavljen — grediše gledat božje lice.
Puk obrazom nice nad greb plačan zarča
Govore': »Danice svitlost nam pomarča,
»Kêno glas potarča slavan po svitu svem
»I nju smart posarča, evo je u grobu sem.
385 »Sama kâ biše prem dostojna živiti
»Za napokonjim dnem svih vikov, svih liti,
»Ojme, da viditi nećemo ju veće,
»Ni s njom govoriti; obrati nam pleće.
»Utišit se neće, Judita, za tobom
390 »Puk ov, jer ležeće neć' ga prijat s sobom,
»Ti s' zaparta grobom, mi suze ronimo,
»Ubijeni smo znobom, ča ćemo, ne vimo.
»Ti nam biše, vimo, utiha pečali,
»A sada kopnimo prez tebe ostali;
395 »Svi smo evo pali kako prisičen bor,
»I veli i mali tebi upije: »Otvor!«
»Otvor, ter nas zatvor s sobom u tom grebi,
»S tobom umriti umor gorak nam jur ne bi,
»Da gorko po tebi živit je življen'je,
400 »Svaki plače sebi da zgubi utišen'je:
»Da zgubi učen'je svake riči prave,
»Da zgubi dičen'je svake s tobom slave.
»Ojme! Da prez glave ostasmo marzal trup,
»Sarce jadi dave, ostasmo pribijen stup.
405 »Ojme! Tko toko tup i tvard more biti,
»Da bijen od tacih krup neće pocviliti
»Ali ustaviti pečalno tužen'je?
»Gdi ste naši svïti, gdi s' naše počten'je?
»Gdi si urešen'je, gdi si naša časti?
410 »Gdi si uzvišen'je izraelske vlasti?
»Gdi si vela slasti svetoga života?
»Gdi s' razuma splasti, gdi s' svaka dobrota?
»Od nas se odmota, a sad ča čekamo,
»Ner da nam teškota nika pride samo!
415 »Prez tebe predamo, prez tebe hoditi
»Ne umimo kamo, ni ča učiniti.

---

381. Kako puk plaka smart Juditinu.

Of the prison of flesh, went to gaze on God's face. 380
The people, bowed low, hasten weeping to the tomb,³¹
Saying: "The brightness of our day star hath grown dark;
Whose fame raced gloriously throughout the world,
And whom death has swallowed, behold she is in
    the grave.
Her who was deemed most worthy to live 385
To the fullness of her age and years,
Alas, we shall see no more,
Nor speak with her; she has turned her back to us.
This people, Judith, mourneth after thee,
For thou who liest here will not take them with thee; 390
Thou art shut up in the grave; we shed tears,
We are smitten with grief, we know not what to do.
We know that thou wast solace in our sorrow,
But now, bereft of thee, we pine away.
Behold, we all have fallen like a cut pinetree, 395
And small and great together beseech thee: 'Open wide!'
Open wide and enclose us with thee in this grave,
Death would not be bitter were we to die with thee;
But bitter it is to live life after thee.
Each weepeth for he hath lost his consolation: 400
He hath lost the wisdom of each of thy words,
He hath lost the merit of all thy praiseworthiness.
Alas, for we have become a cold corpse without a head,
Griefs assail the heart, we have become a ruined column.
Alas, who can be so obtuse or hardhearted 405
That beaten down by such blows he would not wail?
Or leave off his sad mourning?
Where are ye, our counsels, where art thou, our pride?
Where art thou, adornment; where art thou, our honour?
Where art thou, exaltation of Israelite power? 410
Where art thou, great sweetness of a holy life?
Where art thou, mantle of wisdom; where, every good?
Thou hast gone from us, and now, what may we await
Except that some trouble come and strike us anew?
Without thee we give up, without thee we bow down, 415
We know neither the way nor what we might do.

---

31. How the people did lament Judith's death.

»Ti nas zaščititi od zla umijaše,
»Ti nas obraniti od sile mogaše,
»Sunce ti nam sjaše u dne ter u noći,
420   »Dokla ti življaše; — tko će sad pomoći?« —
Timi žutki voći svi se pokladahu,
Take tužbe moći k sarcu privijahu;
Tako žaleć stahu; osmi dan kad pride,
Svi jure mučahu; svak na stan otide.
425   Sila ne izide koja bi zadila
Sela ali zide sinov Izraila,
Dokla je živila Judita na saj svit,
Zemlja je u mir bila i potom vele lit.
Dan u ki bi dobit Oloferne, htiše
430   Svećen'je vazda bit od tih ki dobiše,
Dokla ne podbiše pod jaram svu šiju,
Pokol umoriše s proroci Mesiju.
Komu poklon diju, Bogu, spasu momu,
Jere konac viju počitan'ju tomu,
435   Juditi u komu slava će bit dokol
Svitu zemaljskomu počne gorit okol;
Ako li daj dotol dokla zemlja ova
Bude na karte folj slovinjska čtit slova.
Trudna toga plova ovdi jidra kala
440   Plavca moja nova: Bogu budi hvala,
Ki nebesa skova i svaka ostala.
Amen.

OVDI SVARSUJU KNJIGE
MARKA MARULA SPLICANINA
SVARHU ISTORIJE SVETE UDOVICE JUDITE
NA SVEM BOGU HVALA!

Thou knewest how to protect us from evil,
Thou wert able to defend us from force,
Thou didst shine for us like the sun, day and night,
Whilst thou didst live. Who will now help us?"   420
Upon such bitter fruits did they thus feed,
Sorrows of such magnitude bound they around
    their hearts;
They stood thus mourning; when came the eighth day,
Each held his peace, each went his own way.
No power was ever born that might touch   425
The towns or cities of the children of Israel;
Whilst Judith still lived in this world,
The earth was at peace, and for many years after.
They decreed that the day Holofernes was conquered
Should alway be celebrated by them who had won,   430
Till they did place their necks beneath the yoke
After they had killed with the prophets, Messiah.

This gift I make to God, Who is my salvation,
For I see now the end of my narration,
In the which Judith's glory shall last until   435
The very circle of this earthly world begin to burn;
Or at least for as long a time as this world
Shall on paper read the written Slavic word.
Exhausted from its journey, this new boat of mine
Lowereth now its sails: Praise be to God   440
Who crafted the heavens and everything else.

Amen.

*Here end the folios of Marko Marulic of Split, containing the history of the blessed widow Judith. To God be praise in all things!*